CONTENTS

ILLUSTRATIONS

PREFACE

It is the authors' hope that *To Be a Roman*, a combined textbook/workbook written for younger and beginning Latin students, will help to fill a significant need in the Latin curriculum. Although the study of the Latin language ideally affords students close contact with the culture of the ancient Romans, it is difficult to find an age-appropriate ancillary text offering a systematic approach to the study of daily life in Ancient Rome. *To Be a Roman* aims to simplify the sometimes daunting task of organizing and presenting a wide array of cultural information for teachers and to offer a selection of engaging material, exercises, and activities for students.

Latin teachers are frequently faced with the dilemma of how to incorporate a range of cultural information into the class while adhering to the framework of a language textbook. Although most reading-based Latin textbooks with an imaginative storyline address certain aspects of daily life as the plot of the story unfolds, none offers a broad range of topics accompanied by comprehensive exercises and activities designed specifically to reinforce cultural information.

Designed to accompany any current Latin textbook, *To Be a Roman* presents a variety of practical information topically. Although the material is arranged to suggest a natural and logical flow of ideas and topics, the teacher is not bound to adhere to the ordering of chapters in this book. If, for example, a discussion of slavery or farming harmonizes with information presented early in the language textbook, teachers are encouraged to read these chapters with their students out of sequence.

The first nineteen chapters of cultural material are copiously illustrated, written in language appropriate for younger students, and accompanied by a variety of exercises that includes, among other types, crossword puzzles, word searches, matching columns, true/false questions and fill-in-the-blanks. Also presented are topics for discussion and both small and large group activities that involve role-playing, artistic creativity, and games. The final chapter is comprised of an extensive, annotated, chapter-by-chapter resource guide to films and fiction about ancient Rome.

This book does not attempt to present a systematic history of ancient Rome and it barely touches upon the complexities of Roman government. Nor is it intended to serve as a definitive source or the final word on the cultural practices of the ancient Romans. Instead, *To Be a Roman* offers generally accepted beliefs about the customs and habits of the Romans. The topics comprise a practical body of information, such as: class distinctions, family life, occupations, measuring time and space, leisure activities, public entertainment, and religious practices. Chapters 18 and 19, examining successive stages in the lives of Roman males and females, serve as a summary and a review of information presented in previous chapters.

The authors have endeavored to use current and reliable sources in conducting the research for this book. They are grateful to both LeaAnn Osburn and Andrew Adams, co-editors, for their many helpful corrections and suggestions. Any errors of fact or judgment that may remain are, of course, entirely the responsibility of the authors. Acknowledgement is also due to Christina Huemer, the librarian of the American Academy in Rome as well as to Lavinia Ciuffa, Curatorial Assistant of the Academy's Fototeca Unione, who were both most generous with their time and assistance in helping the authors obtain illustrations. Margaret Brucia acknowledges her indebtedness to her Latin students in Port Jefferson, NY and wishes to thank the University of Washington's Helen R. Whiteley Center, where she spent two happy and productive weeks working on the manuscript of *To Be a Roman*. Greg Daugherty wishes to thank both his wife Cathy (who is a Latin teacher in Hanover County, Virginia) for her invaluable advice and counsel and his students in Classics 225 for helping to pilot much of the content.

MARGARET A. BRUCIA
GREGORY N. DAUGHERTY

August 21, 2006

CHAPTER 1:
ROMAN SOCIETY

SLAVES, FREEDMEN, AND PLEBEIANS

The Romans, like other ancient civilizations, divided their people into distinct social groups. At the bottom step of the social scale were slaves, who had no rights or privileges whatsoever. But slaves in ancient Rome could, and often did, become legally free. When slaves were granted their freedom, they became known as *libertini*, or freedmen and freedwomen. *Libertini* were eligible for Roman citizenship. Once they became citizens of Rome, they joined the ranks of the lowest and largest class of citizens, the plebeian class. Although the social stigma of having once been a slave remained for freed people, as new citizens they mingled freely with free-born citizens.

THE UPPER CLASSES

Above the plebeian class were those citizens who sprang from distinguished family backgrounds and who usually possessed great wealth. In the earliest period of Roman history there was one upper class, whose membership was determined solely by family background. Gradually a second upper class emerged. The rules for membership in each of the upper classes changed as Rome itself grew in size and importance. In order to understand how and why the upper classes developed, it is helpful to know some background information about Rome's three phases of government: monarchy, republic, and empire.

FROM MONARCHY TO REPUBLIC TO EMPIRE

At first, monarchs or kings ruled Rome. During the Monarchy, some leaders were outstanding and some clearly were not. The traditional dates for the Monarchy are 753–509 BCE. After the seventh and last king, a tyrant, was overthrown, the Romans, fearful of one-man rule, established a republic. The traditional dates for the Republic are 509–27 BCE. Roman citizens now voted for their leaders in elections.

The highest elected official was called a *consul*, and two men, who shared power equally, were elected to this office every year. Citizens who had held public offices were eligible to become senators. The role of the Senate was to give advice to political officials. Although this system of government was effective for many centuries, eventually the Roman Republic began to falter and break apart. Power once again passed to a single man, but this time he was called an emperor instead of a king. The last period of Roman history is therefore known as the Roman Empire. Most of the laws that determined which social class people belonged to were established during the Roman Republic. The traditional dates for the Empire are 27 BCE–476 CE.

American Academy in Rome, Photographic Archive

Fig. 1.
This frieze from the *Ara Pacis*, created in the very early years of the Empire, shows Romans dressed formally in their togas.

PATRICIANS

In the early years of the Roman Republic, class was mainly determined by family background. Just as some Americans today are proud to have in their family tree a Native American, or a Pilgrim who traveled on the Mayflower or a signer of the Declaration of Independence, so Romans boasted about their descent from families whose names and deeds appeared in the earliest histories of Rome. Families who could trace their heritage back to the beginning of Rome became members of the highest class. They were called patricians.

PATRICIANS VS. PLEBEIANS

There were, naturally, far fewer patricians than other members of Roman society. By banding together, however, and supporting their own causes, patricians became so powerful that they soon controlled the rest of the Roman citizens, the plebeians. Although most of the patricians were wealthy, others lost their fortunes as time passed. A few of the plebeians, in the meantime, managed to accumulate great wealth during the growth and development of the Republic. Since money had helped to make the patricians powerful, the newly wealthy plebeians believed that they now deserved a more important and influential role in the emerging Republic.

After a long and bitter struggle against the patricians, plebeians eventually gained the legal right to seek political office. Descent from an ancient and illustrious family, though still important, gradually became less important than wealth in determining a person's social class. Rome was now divided by class and by wealth. There were two social classes, patricians and plebeians, some of whom were rich and some of whom were poor. There was no middle class.

NOBLES AND COMMONERS

By the middle of the republican period, the terms "patrician" and "patrician class" had disappeared. Wealthy citizens, who called themselves "the good men" or "the best men," divided themselves into two groups, politicians and businessmen. Those who chose politics as their career and held a public office became senators, and their families became members of the senatorial class of citizens. On the other hand, those families whose members engaged primarily in business made up the equestrian class. Equestrians, however, were not barred from seeking public office. Indeed, individual members of the equestrian class often did hold elected governmental positions. Once a family member from either class attained the highest public office, that of *consul*, then his family, whether senatorial or equestrian, became noble. It is important to remember that members of both the senatorial and the equestrian class were generally wealthy.

Just as wealthy citizens had different labels, so did the lower class of citizens. During the Republic and onwards, the plebeian class was often referred to as simply "the people" or sometimes "the commoners."

Although the names of social groups were not always consistent, each person's class and social status were absolutely clear to other Romans. And everyone was expected to act in accordance with his or her place in society. Three clues that immediately indicated a person's social class and standing were: clothing, name, and the name of one's patron.

CLOTHING

The first and most obvious clue was clothing. Only citizens were permitted to wear a toga over their tunic. Of course the quality and expense of the toga provided a further indication of the wearer's status. Furthermore, senators and equestrians wore distinctive purple stripes on their togas and tunics, broad

Fig. 2.
Notice the difference between the nobles wearing togas and the attendant wearing a tunic and cloak.

stripes for senators and narrow ones for equestrians. They were also allowed to wear special rings and accessories. The way they dressed instantly set toga-clad senators, equestrians, and plebeians apart from the tunic-clad masses of slaves and from foreigners. A poor citizen probably owned only one toga, but he wore it whenever he needed to assert his status as a Roman citizen. Women's clothing, on the other hand, did not indicate their rank as clearly as men's clothing did.

NAMES

The second clue to a person's class was his or her name. Names revealed much information about status. It was common, but by no means the rule, for upper-class males to have a three-part name. Julius Caesar's full name, for example, was Caius Julius Caesar. The first name in this series, Caius (also spelled Gaius), was called the *praenomen* and was equivalent to a first name, such as Michael, or David, or Paul. The second name, Julius, was called the *nomen*, and it identified the extended family or clan. The third name, Caesar, was called the *cognomen*. This name was most commonly used to indicate the branch of the family to which the person belonged.

There was a limited number of male *praenomina*, and only 15 routinely appear: Aulus, Caius, Cnaius (also spelled Gnaeus), Decimus, Kaeso, Lucius, Manius, Marcus, Publius, Quintus, Servius, Sextus, Spurius, Tiberius, and Titus. These names were usually abbreviated: A., C., Cn., D., K., L., M'., M., P., Q., Ser., Sex., S., Ti., and T. Women rarely had *praenomina*. Well-established families customarily limited their choice of *praenomina* to a few names and bestowed them in a set order. The Julian family, for example, named their sons Caius, Lucius, and Sextus, in that order. It was usually clear from his name who was the first-born son and heir.

Everyone had at least a *nomen*, and frequently that was all a woman or a slave had. The majority of male free-born Roman citizens, however, had only two names, a *praenomen* and a *nomen*. There were only a few patrician family *nomina*, and most ended in –ius, such as Julius, Aemilius, Flavius, and Cornelius.

American Academy in Rome, Photographic Archive

Fig. 3.
This tomb was built by Ti. Claudius Eutychus for his wife, Claudia Memonides.

The third name, the *cognomen*, usually marked the branch of the clan, such as the Caesarean branch of the Julian family. In the case of the Cornelian family, on the other hand, the *cognomen* made it possible to distinguish between the patrician members, who used the *cognomen* Lentulus, and the plebeian members, who used the *cognomen* Scipio. *Cognomina* were most common among patrician families and frequently referred to a physical trait, temperament, or origin of the original member of the branch. For example, Albus means "the pale one," Benignus means "the kind one," and Siculus means "the man from Sicily." Cn. Pompeius, a famous rival of Julius Caesar, selected his own cognomen, Magnus, or "The Great."

A fourth name, called an *agnomen* was sometimes added. If a family became excessively large, an *agnomen* could indicate a new branch of the family or a sub-division of a pre-existing branch, as in the name P. Cornelius Scipio Nasica. On rare occasions, an individual earned a fourth name as an honor for a great achievement. P. Cornelius Scipio Africanus, for example, acquired the name "Africanus" after his defeat of Hannibal in Africa.

Adoption was common in ancient Rome. Fathers without sons frequently adopted young men from other families so that they could leave their property and wealth, as an inheritance, to the next generation of their family. An adopted son assumed the full name of his adoptive father, but kept his original *nomen* with the addition of a new suffix, *–anus*. When L. Aemilius Paullus was adopted by P. Cornelius Scipio, for example, he became P. Cornelius Scipio Aemilianus. Thus it was clear to all who met him that he had been adopted.

Women were known only by the feminine form of their *nomen*, so Caesar's only daughter was named Julia. If Caesar had more daughters, they would all have been named Julia. To eliminate confusion, sisters sometimes attached to their *nomen* additional names that meant "the older" or "the younger," or "second" or "third." Thus, if Caesar had had two daughters, they might have been known as Julia Major and Julia Minor. If he had had three daughters, they might have been called Julia, Julia Secunda, and Julia Tertia.

Sometimes, when the clan was exceptionally large, the *cognomen* of a woman's father was added with the ending changed to show possession. The name Caecilia Metelli, for example, means Caecilia of Metellus. This woman's family was the Metellan branch of the Caecilian family. Diminutives and nicknames were also common, especially among women. The diminutive form of the name Agrippina, for example, was Agrippinilla, and of Livia was Livilla.

Foreigners used their native names. If they were granted Roman citizenship, foreigners usually preserved their native name as a *cognomen* added to the *praenomen* and *nomen* of their patron. For example, a foreigner named Lysidimus, who became a Roman citizen and had a Roman patron named Lucus Caecilius, was known as L. Caecilius Lysidimus.

Slaves were named by their master. Oftentimes these names were foreign, mythological, or descriptive. A slave might be called Cleopatra, or Daedalus, or Glaucus (grey-eyed), for example. If a male slave were freed, like a foreigner, he generally kept his slave name as a *cognomen* added to the *praenomen* and the *nomen* of his former master. Similarly, freedwomen assumed the name of their mistress. And so, a slavewoman named Caenis became known as Antonia Caenis after she was freed. Antonia, the daughter of Marcus Antonius, was the *nomen* of Caenis' former mistress and patron.

PATRONS AND CLIENTS

Discovering the social standing of a citizen's patron provided a third valuable clue to establishing that person's place in society. Most Roman citizens served as a client or supporter of a patron. The more prominent the patron, the more highly regarded was his client. Freedmen of distinguished patrons frequently rose to very high stations.

Patrons selected their clients carefully, and some collected more than a hundred supporters on whom they depended for loyalty and service. Typically, clients were expected to congregate in the morning at the house of their wealthier patron to greet him as soon as he went outdoors to begin his day. If the patron wished, his clients accompanied him on any political or legal business where an impressive and large crowd of supporters might prove useful or beneficial. Clients were the patron's "people." In exchange for this show of support from his clientele, a patron was expected to assist his clients in time of need and to provide them with food, money, or legal assistance.

The system of patronage in Rome can be described as a great pyramid. At the top were the wealthiest citizens who had so much money that they did not need a patron of their own. Below them were their clients who, in turn, could also be patrons to other clients farther down the social scale. And so on, until the base of the pyramid encompassed nearly all the citizens of Rome. A slave who was freed almost always became a client of his former master. The citizens who had no patron were the truly destitute and the homeless who could not qualify to become clients.

The relationship between patron and client was a central feature of Roman social and political life. Violating the mutual trust between a patron and in his client was one of the most serious moral offenses one could commit. These relationships could be initiated at any time, were often inherited, and were rarely canceled.

Obviously there were many other ways a Roman could let others know who he was, how wealthy he was, and where he belonged in Roman society. But these three factors or signals-- clothing, name, and a citizen's client/patron relationship-- were the easiest to observe in a society that not only wanted, but needed to know and to communicate the place each person held in the system.

Chapter 1 Exercises: *Roman Society*

FILL IN THE BLANKS

Use the following word bank to fill in the blanks:

nobles	plebeians	equestrians	patrons	slaves
emperors	senators	patricians	kings	freedmen/freedwomen

1. The non-citizens of Rome who enjoyed no rights or privileges were called _____.

2. Slaves who were granted their freedom were known as _____.

3. Those families who could trace their ancestry back to the earliest days of Rome were called _____.

4. The members of the lowest class of Roman citizens were _____.

5. An upper-class citizen who held a public office was entitled to join a political advisory group made up of _____.

6. Upper-class citizens who engaged in business were called _____.

7. A *consul* and his family members were known as _____.

8. The earliest rulers of Rome were seven _____.

9. During the last phase of Rome's history, Rome was ruled by _____.

10. Clients were expected to show loyal support to their _____.

ABBREVIATIONS AND WORD SEARCH

Write the abbreviation for the *praenomina* listed below. Then find each name in the word search puzzle.

Aulus	_____	Publius	_____
Caius	_____	Quintus	_____
Cnaius	_____	Servius	_____
Decimus	_____	Sextus	_____
Kaeso	_____	Spurius	_____
Lucius	_____	Tiberius	_____
Manius	_____	Titus	_____
Marcus	_____		

L	P	A	T	I	U	M	A	N	I	U	S	L
A	U	L	U	S	P	A	R	L	K	A	T	U
R	B	I	S	P	U	R	I	U	S	D	U	S
S	L	G	N	A	I	C	U	C	R	E	S	E
T	I	B	E	R	I	U	S	I	A	C	K	R
I	U	S	P	Q	R	S	Q	U	N	I	A	V
T	S	Q	U	I	N	T	U	S	U	M	E	I
U	C	A	I	U	S	S	E	X	T	U	S	U
S	E	R	V	I	C	N	A	I	U	S	O	S

WORD STUDY

Match each of the following words in Column A with a word associated with it by derivation in Column B. Explain the connection in the blank provided.

	Column A		Column B	
1. _____	Monarchy	a)	liberty	_____
2. _____	Republic	b)	majority	_____
3. _____	Patron, patrician	c)	consult	_____
4. _____	Nomen	d)	plebiscite	_____
5. _____	Liberti	e)	minus	_____
6. _____	*Consul*	f)	monocle	_____
7. _____	Senator	g)	paternal	_____
8. _____	Major	h)	senile	_____
9. _____	Minor	i)	tertiary	_____
10. _____	Plebeian	j)	publish	_____
11. _____	Secunda	k)	nominate	_____
12. _____	Tertia	l)	secondary	_____

Names

From what you have learned about Roman names, make some observations about the famous Romans listed below. Then, try to find information about each of these people to see if you are correct.

C. Julius Caesar Octavianus Augustus

P. Cornelius Scipio Aemilianus Africanus Minor

M. Tullius Cicero

Tullia

C. Mucius Scaevola

Lucretia

Cloelia

Small Group Project

Three Roman men are engaged in conversation on a busy street corner in Rome near the senate house. All three men are wearing togas. One man, named L. Fabius Eurydicus, a bakery owner, is speaking Latin with a strong Greek accent. Eurydicus, who was born on the Greek island of Crete, is telling C. Oppius, who also owns a bakery, about the new ovens he has just purchased. Oppius, however, is more interested in displaying his new ring to Eurydicus. Both Oppius and Eurydicus are the clients of the third man, L. Fabius Justus, who also wears a large ring on his finger. Fabius' toga has a broad purple stripe. Fabius listens with interest to the conversation of the two men, but soon excuses himself and hurries off toward the senate house, where he is expected to attend a meeting.

1. From the information given above, identify the social class of each man. List as many clues as you can that help you to determine each man's status. Create a plausible biography for each man.

2. Draw a full-length picture of Eurydicus, Oppius and Fabius.

For Discussion

Discuss the pros and cons of the patron/client pyramid in Roman society.

CHAPTER 2: THE FAMILY

The structure of a Roman family was quite different from what we call a nuclear family. Extending beyond father, mother, and children, a Roman family unit, called the *familia*, included several generations of relatives, often living together under the same roof. Slaves and, in the case of farm families, livestock were also considered part of the Roman *familia*, as was a unique set of protective gods and spirits. The *familia* was at the core of the social, religious and political life of Rome.

THE *PATERFAMILIAS*

All of the people, property, and rituals associated with a Roman *familia* came under the authority and guidance of the one supremely important patriarch called the *paterfamilias*. Besides his role as head of the family, the *paterfamilias* was the legal owner of everything and everyone in the household and the guardian of all of its religious rituals.

Fig. 4.
In this wall painting, we see the *paterfamilias* and *materfamilias* sacrificing at an altar accompanied by children and/or slaves.

The *paterfamilias* was the only male in the family who enjoyed full legal rights and protection under Roman law. He, in turn, held legal power over everyone else in the family, including his wife and, of course, their slaves. He was responsible at all times for the welfare and the behavior of his family. A *paterfamilias* had the right to banish, execute, or sell into slavery a family member if he thought the person was guilty of serious misconduct.

DIVORCE

Divorce, though possible, was a complicated procedure if the couple had married according to the strict, old-fashioned custom popular in the earliest days. Most marriages in the late Republic and the Empire were of a less restrictive type. Under the newer measures, divorce was a comparatively easy matter. Either the husband or the wife (or the *paterfamilias* of the wife's original family) could initiate a divorce. To become legally divorced, one needed only to inform the spouse of the intention to divorce. When a divorce took place, the woman traditionally returned to her original family and was placed, once again, under the control of her family's *paterfamilias*. Her children remained in their father's family.

Adoption

Adopting an already grown and healthy male was safer than adopting a young child, since children were more susceptible to death from common childhood diseases. Romans sometimes adopted children, but more often grown men from other families. Adoption guaranteed the survival of the family name and property. Since children were expected to provide financial support for their aging parents, adoption also guaranteed a livelihood for parents of limited economic resources. When a person of any age was adopted, that person came under the authority of the family's *paterfamilias*.

Newborn Babies

When a child was born into a Roman family, the *paterfamilias* decided whether the newborn infant should be accepted into the family. Shortly after the baby's birth, the infant was laid at the feet of the *paterfamilias*. If he picked up the child, he acknowledged it as his legitimate offspring. Sometimes, however, if the infant appeared to be deformed or defective in any way, the *paterfamilias* might refuse to pick up and accept the child. If the *paterfamilias* rejected the baby, the child was exposed. This means that the baby was abandoned, probably at a designated spot. Unwanted children were often taken by strangers or slave dealers.

Sometimes a baby was rejected simply because she was female. Girls were expensive. When a daughter was married, her family was expected to pay a large sum of money, a dowry, to her husband's family for her upkeep in her new family. Having many daughters in a family could cause serious financial hardship, especially for a poor family.

Pietas and *Judicium Domesticum*

While the power of the *paterfamilias* was absolute and his treatment of family members potentially harsh, two practices helped to soften and moderate his behavior. First, Romans believed in and practiced the virtue of *pietas*. Although this word is difficult to define, to a Roman it meant loyalty, obligation, and devotion to the welfare of the *familia* (and to other members of society as well as to the gods). A *paterfamilias* wanted his *familia* to flourish and prosper, and therefore he made decisions that he believed would be good for the *familia* as a whole, as well as for the individual members.

Second, Romans customarily held a family court or council, called a *judicium domesticum* if the *paterfamilias* was considering imposing harsh penalties on a family member. Although the final disciplinary decision remained with the *paterfamilias*, the council provided him with the opportunity to hear the thoughts, opinions, and suggestions of other family members.

Succession to the Role of *Paterfamilias*

When a *paterfamilias* died, each full-grown son gained his independence and could become a *paterfamilias* to his own sons and daughters, and eventually to his sons' children. On the other hand, those sons who had not come of age before the death of their *paterfamilias* and any unmarried daughters, no matter what their age, were placed under the guardianship of a person previously chosen by the *paterfamilias* and named in his will. If a *paterfamilias* died without appointing a guardian for his younger sons and unmarried daughters, a public official assigned a guardian until the sons came of age and the daughters were married.

It was most unusual for a Roman male to assume the role of *paterfamilias* while his own father was still alive. To do so, the man first had to be legally free from his father's control. This happened, for example, in the unlikely event that his father was banished or stripped of his citizenship for political reasons, or if he was declared incapable of performing the functions of a *paterfamilias*. At certain times, however, a man could become temporarily free of the control of his *paterfamilias*. If a Roman became the high-priest of Jupiter or one of the top government officials, for example, he was free, but only for the duration of the term of his priesthood or office.

THE FAMILY AND FOREIGNERS

Only Roman families were bound by this complicated type of family structure. Foreigners living under Roman law did not have such rights over their descendants. Like the toga that he wore and the family gods that watched over him, the *paterfamilias* was uniquely Roman.

FEMALES

Unfortunately, the rights and restrictions of Roman women are not so well documented as those of Roman men. We do know, however, that the wife of the *paterfamilias*, known as the *materfamilias*, had comparatively few legal rights. Rome was clearly a patriarchal and male-dominated society. We have seen that female children suffered a higher rate of exposure than male children, brides were forced to leave their families and to obey their husband and his *paterfamilias*, and widows were sometimes placed under the control of their sons. Wives were frequently much younger than their first husbands.

Motherhood was considered the primary role of a Roman woman, and mothers were respected and revered by every member of Roman society. Although affection was often expressed by husbands towards their wives and vice versa, the real purpose of marriage was to produce children. A married woman, known as a *matrona*, who did not produce offspring was usually divorced and returned to her family with her dowry.

Fig. 5.
A Roman matron was expected to act modestly and bear children.

A matron with sons, on the other hand, earned the respect of Roman society. If she had been married only once and enjoyed a virtuous reputation, her respectability increased. Skill in managing the household and making clothing were more valuable assets for a woman than a good education. By most modern standards, Roman girls and women led quiet lives, with their tasks restricted to maintenance of the house and family.

CHILDREN

Children were essential to the survival of the Roman family and to the passing on of the family's name, property, and household gods to the next generation. Roman women usually gave birth to their children at home, with the assistance of a midwife and well-trained slaves. Infants remained nameless for the first few days of their life, when they were most susceptible to complications from birth and to fatal childhood diseases. On the ninth day for boys, the eighth for girls, a purification ceremony and the *Nominalia*, at which the child received a name, were held. The newborn baby received a distinctive necklace decorated with rattles. The noise of the rattles was intended to scare away evil spirits. As the infant became a toddler, the noise of the rattles helped grownups locate a child on the move.

The *paterfamilias* gave the child a *bulla*, a hollow, round, and somewhat puffy, locket. Made of metal, cloth or leather, the *bulla* was suspended on a string fastened around the child's neck. Inside the *bulla* was a protective amulet or charm. A girl wore her *bulla* until her wedding day, and a boy stopped wearing his on the day of his coming-of-age ceremony.

American Academy in Rome, Photographic Archive

Fig. 6.
Around the neck of this child hangs his *bulla,* a distinctively shaped protective charm.

Aside from their education we know very little about the lives of Roman children. In wealthier families, young children were often attended to by both a nurse and a male slave called a *paedagogus,* who took care of them and made sure that they learned their lessons.

Many children's toys, dolls, balls, and game pieces have been found by archaeologists or are depicted in art. Most of them are basic toys not unlike those still in use today. They indicate that simple, imaginative play was a common feature of Roman childhood. Although it is difficult to make generalizations, lower class children probably entered the work force as soon as they were physically able, whereas wealthy Roman boys were expected to enter public life and military service during their late teens and early twenties. Ideally, girls were married during their early teenage years.

SLAVES

Slaves were part of the Roman *familia.* Household slaves contributed in a special way to everyday life. In a wealthy household, for example, some slaves acted as personal attendants who helped their masters and mistresses dress and groom themselves each day, some minded or nursed the children, still others served as cooks, house cleaners, secretaries, night watchmen, and body guards. Even the poorest household normally had one or two slaves. Domestic slaves usually received preferential treatment.

SUMMARY

And so we have seen that a Roman *familia* was multi-generational and included slaves, and often live-stock. The *paterfamilias*, its all-powerful authority figure, controlled every aspect of the lives of those in the family. Married women could be divorced and returned to their original family. Unmarried women and underage sons were always under the watchful eye of an authority figure, either their *paterfamilias* or a guardian. Little is known about the day-to-day activities of children. The Roman *familia*, when it functioned properly, was like a well-oiled machine, with each member performing specific tasks. The result was a strong family unit that continued to prosper with each succeeding generation.

American Academy in Rome, Photographic Archive

Fig. 7.
This tomb relief depicts a husband and wife clasping hands and gazing at each other tenderly.

Chapter 2 Exercises: *The Family*

TRUE OR FALSE

Indicate whether each statement is true or false. If it is false, identify the error and correct it.

1. _____   Slaves and farm animals were considered part of a Roman family.

2. _____   The *paterfamilias* and the *materfamilias* had equal authority over the family.

3. _____   The *paterfamilias*, his sons, and their sons enjoyed full legal rights and protection under Roman law.

4. _____   A *paterfamilias* could banish or execute a member of the family, but even he could not sell a family member into slavery.

5. _____   Roman wives were not permitted to initiate a divorce.

6. _____   A divorced woman usually returned to live with her original family.

7. _____   Once a Roman child came of age, he was no longer eligible for adoption.

8. _____   Adult male children were expected to provide financial security for their elderly parents.

9. _____   A newly married woman had to live with her husband's family and obey his *paterfamilias*, but an adopted son could choose the family with whom he would live.

10. _____   Newborn babies were placed on the ground at the feet of their mother.

11. _____   Infants were sometimes left outside to die because they were born with birth defects.

12. _____   When a daughter was married, her father received a payment from her husband's family.

13. _____   *Pietas* was the act of punishing a family member harshly.

14. _____   A *judicium domesticum* enabled the *paterfamilias* to hear the thoughts of his family members before he made an important decision.

15. _____   When a *paterfamilias* died, all of his sons and daughters were placed under the control of appointed guardians.

16. _____   If a *paterfamilias* became ill, his sons were free of their father's control for the duration of his illness.

17. _____   Foreigners living under Roman rule were not bound by the same rules that applied to Roman families.

18. _____   We know as much about the rights and privileges of Roman women as we do about Roman men.

19. _____   For the Romans, the primary role of marriage was to produce offspring.

20. _____   It was considered beneath the dignity of a Roman woman to make clothing with her own hands.

21. _____   Roman women normally went to a clinic to give birth to their children.

22. _____ It was customary to name a Roman child on the day of his or her birth.

23. _____ The primary function of a baby rattle was to distract and amuse the child.

24. _____ The *bulla* was a protective charm worn by girls and boys until the day they were married.

25. _____ Unfortunately, no children's toys have survived from the ancient world.

26. _____ Only the wealthiest Roman families could afford to have slaves.

SMALL GROUP PROJECTS

1. Imagine a typical multi-generational Roman family in which the *paterfamilias* has just died. How would his death affect the status of each person listed below?

    Adult son with wife and children

    Adopted son

    Underage son

    Unmarried daughter

    Grandchild

    Slave

2. The *paterfamilias* of the Cornelius family has just learned that his son has stolen a large sum of money from a neighboring family. The *paterfamilias* intends to punish his son for damaging his family's reputation.

    A *judicium domesticum* is in progress, during which family members discuss their views as the *paterfamilias* listens. The speakers are:

    Materfamilias: Aemilia

    Older son: C. Cornelius

    Younger son (the thief): M. Cornelius

    Older sister: Cornelia

    Younger sister: Cornelia Minor

    Empedocles: the *paedagogus*

    Write a dialogue or perform a skit in which each family member listed above expresses his or her opinion about how and why Marcus should be punished.

    Pretend you are a modern courtroom artist and draw the *judicium domesticum* in progress.

FOR DISCUSSION

List some of the advantages of living in a multi-generational home setting.

CHAPTER 3:
THE RELIGIOUS RITUALS OF THE FAMILY

INTRODUCTION

Throughout the ages, people of different societies and cultures have celebrated transitions to a new stage of human growth or development. These transitions are known as passages, and the ceremonies that mark them are called rites of passage. In any society, rites of passage almost always mark the birth of a baby, the transformation of a child into a young adult, the union of two adults in marriage, and the death of a person of any age. This chapter will examine the Roman customs associated with these four rites of passage: birth, puberty, marriage, and death.

BIRTH RITES

A *paterfamilias* wanted his *familia* to grow and flourish. Childlessness both jeopardized the continuance of the family to the next generation and brought disgrace to the *paterfamilias*. If no sons and heirs were produced, it was not unusual for a Roman man to divorce his childless wife and marry a new and presumably more fertile woman, or to remarry in the event of his wife's death.

Complications of pregnancy and childbirth were leading causes of death among women. Midwives assisted the wealthy with the delivery, but doctors were summoned only as a last resort. Although Caesarean births were sometimes performed, the mother rarely survived the operation. A woman in labor understandably kept good luck charms about her and prayed for a safe delivery. She and her family made offerings to many gods, but especially to Juno, the patron goddess of women in childbirth.

When a child was successfully born, the rituals of birth began immediately. Three men, impersonating gods, swept the doorway of the family's house with a broom, pounded on the door itself with a pestle, and struck it with an axe. The three items used in the doorway—broom, pestle, and axe—are all tools of a civilized society. As such, they symbolize the civilized world. The still uncivilized child within the house needed the protection of a strong door to keep away the threats of an uncivilized world outside until the child was officially accepted by the *paterfamilias* as a member of the family.

Acceptance into the family was the purpose of the next ritual. The newborn was placed naked on the ground at the feet of the *paterfamilias*. If the *paterfamilias* picked up the baby, the child was immediately accepted as a member of the family and was given a protective amulet or charm, called a *bulla*, to wear around the neck. If, on the other hand, the *paterfamilias* refused to pick up the child, usually because the child had a physical defect or was female, the baby was exposed. This means that the child was abandoned, usually at a designated spot, to die. Sometimes abandoned or exposed children were taken in by others and raised as slaves.

The child in the family remained nameless for the first week of its life. During this period of time, a ceremonial table was set, spread with food, and dedicated to protective gods: to Juno if the child was a girl, or to Hercules if the child was a boy.

The next birth rite, a naming ceremony called the *Nominalia*, occurred on the eighth day after the birth of a girl and on the ninth day after the birth of a boy. This ceremony took place in the presence of the immediate family, relatives, friends, and household slaves. A female child received one name, the feminine form of her father's family name. An upper class male child usually received a first name (*praenomen*), followed by his family name (*nomen*), and sometimes a third name, indicating the branch of the family into which he was born (*cognomen*). The child was now a full and legitimate member of the family.

Children were often given a necklace of rattles and ornaments called a *crepundia*. The noise of the *crepundia* was thought to protect children by scaring away evil spirits and might also prove useful in helping to locate wandering toddlers.

American Academy in Rome

Fig. 8.
This marble sculpture depicts a sleeping child wearing a traveler's hood and holding a lantern.

RITES OF PUBERTY

Puberty, the transition from childhood to adulthood, is a gradual process, marked by a series of physical and emotional changes. For girls, the process is complete whenever they are physically able to bear children. Since childbearing was the primary goal of marriage, the Roman marriage ceremony also served as a rite of puberty for a Roman female. Because the moment of a boy's maturation is more difficult to determine, Romans chose an appropriate day to celebrate a boy's coming of age, usually when he was between the ages of 14 and 17.

A boy's coming-of-age ceremony could take place at any time of the year, but the most popular day for celebrating the event was on the festival of the *Liberalia*, a feast associated with the god Bacchus, on March 17. In the house and in the presence of his whole family, the young man shed the symbols of his childhood: his bordered toga and his *bulla*. He removed his *bulla* and placed it on the family altar along with the first scrapings of his beard as an offering to the household gods. He then put on the plain white toga of an adult male citizen. Then, dressed in his new white toga, he set out for the Forum with his family members, their slaves, and their freedmen and clients. In the Forum he was officially enrolled as an adult citizen eligible to vote.

THREE TYPES OF MARRIAGE RITES

There were three different types of marriage, each bearing its own set of rules and requirements. The strictest type was called *confarreatio*. Under the terms of *confarreatio*, a husband obtained absolute control over his wife. Divorce was not permitted, except in extraordinary circumstances.

During the Republic, *confarreatio* fell out of favor and eventually gave way to another type of marriage called *coemptio*. The Latin word *coemptio* means "a purchase." During this type of ceremony, the groom, placing a coin on a scale, symbolically bought his wife. Although she was expected to obey him, she had more legal rights than someone married under *confarreatio*.

Usus, the third type of marriage and the simplest of the three, was most common among the plebeians. The bride and groom merely joined hands in front of witnesses and declared that they were now husband and wife. As in marriage by *coemptio*, a woman married under the terms of *usus* maintained some personal rights and could obtain a divorce more easily.

No matter which type of marriage rite a couple chose, there were certain requirements for any marriage to be legal. Both the bride and the groom had to have attained puberty, both families had to give consent, and neither could be currently married or too closely related by blood.

THE BETROTHAL

Normally, marriages began with a betrothal. Betrothal was a legal contract between the *paterfamilias*, parents, or guardians of the couple. A handshake in front of witnesses was all that was needed to make a betrothal legal, but written contracts were often drawn up. Sometimes the bride and groom to be were just infants when their betrothal was formalized by their families. Sometimes the bride and groom met each other for the first time on their wedding day.

WEDDING TRADITIONS

Most of the traditions associated with Roman marriage rites trace their origins to the more formal *confarreatio* ceremony. Roman weddings were lengthy and formal events, although few Roman ceremonies included all of the traditions described below.

The wedding day was chosen carefully. Nearly a third of the days in the Roman calendar were considered unlucky, and these days, of course, were avoided. June, the month of Juno, the patron of marriage and childbirth, was the preferred month for the ceremony. On the eve of her wedding day, the bride dedicated her *bulla*, toys, and childhood clothing to the household gods on the family altar. This served as her rite-of-puberty ceremony. That night she slept in a special tunic made of wool and woven in one piece, which she also wore during her wedding ceremony. On the morning of the wedding, the bride's mother helped her dress and fastened a woolen belt around her tunic in a special knot called the knot of Hercules. Only her husband was permitted to untie it.

The bride's hairdo was special and distinctive. Her hair was divided into six sections by the tip of a spear. Each section was then braided and tied with ribbons. She adorned her head with a wreath of flowers that she had gathered. Next, her head was covered with a yellow-orange veil called the *flammeum*. The groom, far more simply clad, wore a toga.

The ceremony itself took place in the house of the bride's father. Before the ceremony began, an animal, usually a sheep, was sacrificed. The meat was then cooked and was often served at the wedding feast.

In the *usus* ceremony, the couple joined hands in the presence of witnesses. In the *coemptio* ceremony, as we have mentioned, the bridegroom placed a coin on a scale in the presence of five witnesses and asked the bride whether she wished to become his *materfamilias*. After she assented, she asked her spouse if he wished to become her *paterfamilias*. Once the groom agreed, they were officially married.

The *confarreatio* was a far more elaborate affair. The bride was accompanied by two ceremonial figures, a matron, called a *pronuba*, and a young boy called a *camillus*. The matron, who had to be still married to her first and only husband, served as the bride's friend and helper. The *camillus*, both of whose parents had to be alive, carried the sacrificial objects and assisted in the sacrifice of the sheep.

The couple was then seated on stools covered with the pelt of the sacrificed sheep. In front of ten witnesses from the patrician order, the bride repeated the formula that served as their wedding vow, "*Ubi tu Gaius, ego Gaia*" (Where you are Gaius, I am Gaia). A cake made of grain, was offered to the gods, and the guests congratulated the couple with the greeting "*feliciter!*"

Often a wedding feast took place at the house where the couple was married. Guests were served a special cake made of fresh grape juice, known as *mustaceum*. As evening approached, the groom pretended to take the bride by force from her mother's embrace. This action was performed so the household gods would not think that the bride was deserting them willingly. The singing of a wedding song and an elaborate torchlight procession to the groom's house followed.

During the procession, the bride continued to wear her *flammeum* for protection, since she had no family gods of her own until she arrived at her husband's house. As further protection, three boys, carrying torches in front of the bride, escorted her. Behind her were other attendants carrying symbols of married life, the spindle and the distaff—objects used to spin and weave wool. The guests followed, singing songs designed to tease and embarrass the couple in a friendly way. The bride carried with her three coins, one for the gods of the crossroads, one for the household gods of her new family, and one for her husband. The groom threw gifts, usually nuts, to the crowds that gathered along the way.

When the procession arrived at the groom's house, he entered first. The bride, after smearing the doorway with wool soaked in oil and fat, was lifted over the threshold. Her husband greeted her inside the house and presented her with fire and water. She lit and then extinguished the family hearth and threw the wood from the hearth to the guests. Next, the *pronuba* removed the bride's *flammeum* and led her to the wedding bed, which had been set up in the entryway of the house. The guests departed. On the next day, there was sometimes a second feast at the house of the groom.

Although the scale was used only in the *coemptio* ceremony, and the grain cake only in the *confarreatio* ceremony, the other customs were freely used in all three ceremonies.

American Academy in Rome, Photographic Archive

Fig. 9.
This man and woman clasp hands in a gesture of affection.

American Academy in Rome, Photographic Archive

Fig. 10.
The sarcophagus containing the bodies of this couple depicts them both together in the central medallion and looking towards each other on either side.

DEATH RITES

Just as upper class Romans planned elaborate marriages, so they conducted extravagant funerals. Not much information survives about the nature of funeral ceremonies for the lower class. The plebeians commonly joined burial clubs and, when they died, the members of the club provided them with a modest funeral. Funeral rites for infants of all classes were brief, and slaves had no ceremonies at all. What follows is a description of the funeral of a typical Roman senator. Other members of the upper classes, including women, might have had a simplified version of this type of funeral.

The senator died at home and his oldest son confirmed his death by leaning over his father's body and calling his father's name. He had already kissed his father on the mouth in an effort to catch his father's last breath. The senator's body was now prepared for burial. First, his eyes were closed. Next, he is bathed and a wax impression of his face is taken. Then his body was dressed in his finest toga with all the insignia of his rank and office visible. His corpse was now arranged on a funeral couch (or seated in a chair) in the entryway of the house and surrounded with flowers and incense. His feet were pointed toward the door, which was festooned with pine or cypress boughs as a warning that the house was polluted by death. (The custom of placing a coin on the dead person's mouth to pay Charon, the ferryman in the Underworld, was rarely practiced in the late Republic and early Empire.) The body remained on view at home for three to seven days. If the body had been embalmed, it would remain on view longer. Embalming, however, was a rare and expensive procedure.

Fig. 11.
A funeral monument on the Via Appia with portraits of those commemorated.

Since corpses had to be buried or cremated beyond the city limits, even a poor man could expect some sort of procession to his tomb. No matter how elaborate or simple the funeral procession was, it served as a notice to the community that someone had died. After a crier announced that the senator's funeral procession was about to begin, his corpse was removed from the house, feet first, so that his ghost would not be able to find its way back inside. Neighbors often joined in the mourning or avoid the pollution of contact with death.

The funeral procession featured musicians and singers of sad, slow songs called dirges. Female professional mourners, who were trained and hired to wail, beat their breasts, scratch their faces, and tear out their hair, stirred the emotions of the attendees. Jesters and mimes performed and relieved the tension. Actors wearing death masks and insignia of the senator's ancestors preceded the body in the procession. The senator himself, with his face exposed, was carried on his couch. Behind him marched his family, including his ex-slaves and slaves. At the end of the procession were torchbearers, reminders of the earlier tradition of burial at night.

The senator's procession entered the Forum and halted in front of the *Rostra*, a stage-like structure used as a speaker's platform. The senator's brother, at the invitation of the family, delivered a funeral oration in the senator's honor.

At the burial site three things occurred. First, the area was consecrated with a sacrificed animal, usually a pig. The mourners consumed the roasted remains of the sacrificed animal and other food provided by the family. Second, earth was placed on the senator's remains. Romans, like people today, practiced both bodily inhumation and cremation. (If the senator had been cremated, a symbolic piece of bone was buried at this point. His ashes were cooled, dried, and preserved elsewhere.) Third, the mourners were sprinkled three times with water for purification.

The family then returned home and made sacrifices to the household gods to request them to purify the house from the taint of death. There followed a nine-day period of grieving, ending with a sacrifice, a banquet, and the distribution of the senator's inheritance.

Funeral games were traditionally held in honor of important citizens. They often included contests similar to track-and-field events. Sometimes slaves, trained as gladiators, fought to the death. These games and contests were held immediately or could be delayed and held as a memorial service several years later.

The period of mourning usually continued for the next ten months. The family continued to commemorate the senator's memory by bringing flowers and food to his tomb on his birth and death days, but especially during the festival of the *Parentalia*, the feast in honor of the ancestors, that was celebrated during the month of February.

Chapter 3 Exercises: *The Religious Rituals of the Family*

Across

6. Wedding cake served to guests
7. The strictest form of marriage
10. Material from which a bride's wedding tunic was made
12. The most common type of marriage among plebeians
13. Attaining adulthood
15. Sad, slow, mournful song
17. A necklace of rattles and ornaments
18. Burning the dead body until it turned to ash
19. The practice of burying the dead in the ground
20. The February festival in honor of the ancestors

Down

1. Marriage by 'purchasing' a wife
2. The yellow-orange wedding veil
3. An amulet or charm given to an infant by the *paterfamilias*
4. The patron of marriage and childbirth
5. He carried the sacred objects used in animal sacrifice
8. Congratulations!
9. Ceremonies that mark human transitions
11. A leading cause of death among women in ancient Rome
14. A legal contract setting down the terms of marriage
16. The Roman equivalent to a Matron-of-Honor

SHORT ANSWERS

Answer the following questions in the space provided.

1. Who was the god who protected infant boys? Who was the goddess who protected infant girls?

2. How were the *bulla* and the *crepundia* similar?

3. When did a girl's coming-of-age ceremony take place?

4. On the day of his coming-of-age ceremony, where did the boy and his family go? What did he do there?

5. Rank the three types of Roman marriages according to their restrictiveness, beginning with the least restrictive.

6. During the marriage ceremony, a Roman bride repeated the sentence, "*Ubi tu Gaius, ego Gaia.*" What is the significance of this declaration?

7. In what two ways did the Romans dispose of the dead bodies of their loved ones?

FOR DISCUSSION

1. Immediately after the birth of a child, three men, impersonating gods, swept the doorway of the house and beat on the door with a pestle and an axe in an effort to ward off the evil influences of an uncivilized world. Discuss what aspects of civilized society a broom, a pestle, and an axe might symbolize. What objects might our society use to symbolize these same three aspects?

2. The *bulla* was a protective charm. What charms do people today use for protection from harm?

3. What sorts of coming-of-age ceremonies do people in America practice? In other countries and cultures?

4. Think about a modern American marriage ceremony. What customs can you think of that are similar to Roman customs? What about marriage customs in other countries and cultures?

5. Why do you think Romans buried their dead outside the city limits?

GROUP PROJECT

Reenact a Roman wedding or funeral, incorporating as many rituals as you wish. Perform your wedding or funeral ceremony live in class, videotape it, or create a computerized slide show using digital images.

CHAPTER 4:
ROMAN HOUSING

INTRODUCTION

There were almost as many types of houses and living quarters in ancient Rome as there are in America today. Although region and setting played an important role in determining style and form, there were three basic types of Roman dwellings: *domus*, *insula*, and *villa*. Whereas the *domus* was a detached or semi-detached town house, the *insula* was an apartment or tenement building. The size and quality of each structure varied enormously, as, of course, did its decoration. This chapter will concentrate on the two types of urban dwellings characteristic of the city of Rome, the *domus* and the *insula*. The *villa* was a rural homestead and will be discussed in a later chapter.

ROOMS OF A ROMAN HOUSE

The *atrium*, the first room one entered, was a reception room. It was here that the master and mistress of the house greeted and welcomed their guests. Its two most conspicuous features were the *compluvium* and the *impluvium*. The *compluvium* was a rectangular opening in the roof designed to admit light and air and to channel rainwater into the *impluvium*, the pool below.

The *tablinum* was the master's den or office. Here he kept the important papers and documents pertaining to the household. The *tablinum* normally opened onto an internal, open-air garden surrounded by a sheltered and colonnaded walkway called the *peristylium*.

Fig. 12.
An opening in the roof was above the shallow pool in the middle of the atrium of this house in Herculaneum.

Protected from sun or rain, family members and guests could sit or stroll and enjoy the well-tended plants and flowers in the central garden.

Food was prepared in a kitchen called the *culina*. Since slaves prepared the meals, the *culina* was strictly a functional workroom with an open hearth and a charcoal stove. It was not elaborately decorated. Slaves served meals in a formal dining room called a *triclinium*. Romans dined on sloping couches positioned around three sides of a small table on which pre-cut, bite-sized pieces of

American Academy in Rome, Photographic Archive

Fig. 13.
This *peristylium*, a colonnaded garden, is in a Roman house in Pompeii.

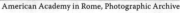

food were placed on serving dishes. Typically, each couch was designed to accommodate three diners, for a total of nine reclining diners. Larger houses frequently contained more than one *triclinium*. Because Romans also enjoyed dining in the open air, a portion of the *peristylium* was often reserved for outdoor meals.

A bedroom was called a *cubiculum* and each was small and simply furnished. Oftentimes a sleeping couch was set into an alcove. Occasionally a small space adjacent to the *cubiculum* offered a place for a slave to wait on call.

Roman houses also included such rooms and features as a *bibliotheca*, or library, where scrolls were kept in pigeonholed shelving along the walls. Some houses had a *vestibulum* (sometimes called *fauces*), an entryway between the street and the *atrium*. Here clients waited to greet their patron as he left his house in the morning, and

Fig. 14.
The heat of the volcanic eruption carbonized this sleeping couch in Herculaneum. It would have been covered with cushions and pillows in ancient times.

here those participating in ritual processions for ceremonies such as coming-of-age ceremonies, funerals, or weddings assembled. Some of the more extravagant private homes had a *latrina*, or toilet. This was typically a small and simple "bench" under which running water flowed to remove the waste.

THE *DOMUS*

A *domus* was a home for the wealthy. It was usually devoid of external ornamentation, but elaborately decorated within. Street frontage was regularly rented out as shops.

Fig. 15.
This model of the remains of a house in Pompeii shows the typical layout of an atrium-style house.

The arrangement of rooms in the *domus* provided for a healthy circulation of fresh air and an abundance of light from the *atrium* and the *peristylium* to the other rooms of the house. The very strong axis or straight path through the *vestibulum*, *atrium*, and *tablinum* is a consistent feature of nearly every *domus*. Sometimes a *triclinium* was also located near this axis. Because these were public spaces where visitors were received and entertained, the rooms were lavishly decorated with frescoes, mosaics, statuary, and fountains. It was important to a Roman homeowner to impress callers. The rooms in the remaining area of the *domus*, intended for private use by the family, showed far more variety in their arrangement and decoration.

The *Insula*

Since space in the city was scarce and expensive, it is not surprising that multi-story, multi-family apartment buildings called *insulae* sprang up in Rome. In fact, the majority of Romans lived in *insulae*. These structures could be six or seven stories tall. As a precaution against fire, a 60-foot height limit was imposed on their construction.

Fig. 16.
This large *insula*, known as the "House of Diana," occupied an entire block in the Roman seaport of Ostia (see Fig. 18).

Fig. 17.
These are the remains of benches in a latrine at Ostia. There were separate facilities for men and women, but no individual cubicles for privacy.

Insulae were built around a central courtyard that provided light and air to the interior units. The ground floor contained shops and sometimes a source of water for cooking and cleaning, and perhaps a *latrina*. Choice units were those on the ground floor, since they provided easy access to water and did not require a long climb. Apartments on the upper stories, reached by steep flights of stairs and prone to the dangers of fire from chimneys, were the least desirable.

Most of the tenants of *insulae* were not members of upper-class society, but neither were they necessarily poor. There was probably a wide spectrum of *insulae*, ranging from the quite comfortable dwellings to buildings that were not well equipped and rather dilapidated.

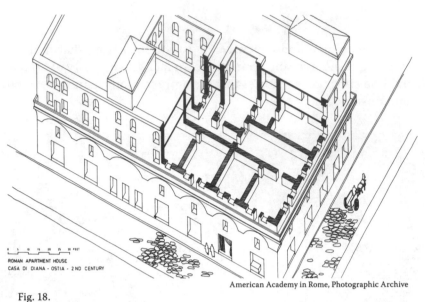

ROMAN APARTMENT HOUSE
CASA DI DIANA - OSTIA - 2ND CENTURY

American Academy in Rome, Photographic Archive

Fig. 18.
Above is a diagram of House of Diana in Ostia (see Fig. 16).

HOUSEHOLD GODS

Almost every Roman house or apartment featured a family shrine. Sometimes a shrine was located in a small niche in a wall, or sometimes it was a freestanding structure. Shrines were placed in many parts of the house, although usually in private spaces. Among other deities, Romans worshipped distinctive gods known as *Lares* and *Penates*, the guardian spirits who protected the welfare and prosperity of each Roman family and its possessions. Many small bronze statuettes of *Lares* have survived. *Penates*, however, who were worshipped at hearth fires and whose specific concern was the family's food supply, were not depicted.

Fig. 19.
The *Lar Familiaris,* worshipped as a protective spirit of the *familia,* was dressed in a simple tunic and carried a cornucopia and a *patera* or dish used in sacrifices.

FURNITURE AND DECORATION

Because only a few examples of Roman furniture have survived from antiquity, wall paintings are our best source of information about Roman décor. Three-legged tables were popular, probably due to their stability on uneven mosaic floors. Cupboards, boxes, and chests, similar in design to their modern counterparts, were common. Chairs, with and without arms, stools, some of which were collapsible, and simple benches provided seating. Sleeping beds and lounging couches, similar in form to each other, were cushioned with mattresses and liberally strewn with pillows.

Upper-class houses were decorated with elaborate frescoes, or wall paintings, and floor mosaics, but also featured movable carved or painted screens and tapestries. The prevalence of live plants and bowls of fruit in wall paintings may indicate that Romans accessorized with fruit and foliage.

Because interior decoration was costly, slave quarters and the living spaces of the lower classes were usually quite plain and monochromatic.

Chapter 4 Exercises: *Roman Housing*
N.B.

Many of the terms used in this chapter are Latin words. In Latin, singular words ending in *–um* form their plural in *–a*, and singular words ending in *–a* form their plural in *–ae*. So, *cubiculum* (bedroom) is singular, but *cubicula* (bedrooms) is plural. Similarly, *latrina* (toilet) is singular, but *latrinae* (toilets) is plural.

FILL IN THE BLANKS

Use the following word bank to fill in the blanks:

peristylium	*atrium*	*compluvium*	*tablinum*
impluvium	*culina*	*cubiculum*	*latrina*
triclinium	*bibliotheca*	*vestibulum*	*fauces*

1. The sparsely furnished sleeping room was called the _____.

2. Important documents and records were kept in the _____.

3. The decorative interior pool located near the entrance of the house was called the _____.

4. In this workroom, known as the _____, slaves prepared the food.

5. Some houses had a room with scrolls shelved along the walls called a _____.

6. Through a system of drainage spouts, rainwater was directed from the _____ to the pool below.

7. Some Roman houses had a private facility for disposing of human waste material called a _____.

8. To sit, chat, and enjoy the garden, Romans spent time in the _____.

9. Romans arranged dining couches around a small table in the _____.

10. The room that contained both the *compluvium* and the *impluvium* was the _____.

11. The _____ (sometimes called _____) was an entryway between the street and the *atrium* where vistors waited and those participating in ceremonies assembled.

Word Study

Match each of the following terms with a word associated by derivation and explain the connection:

1. _____ *bibliotheca*	a) culinary	_____
2. _____ *cubiculum*	b) tablet	_____
3. _____ *insula*	c) Bible	_____
4. _____ *peristylium*	d) trio	_____
5. _____ *domus*	e) insular	_____
6. _____ *tablinum*	f) perimeter	_____
7. _____ *triclinium*	g) domestic	_____
8. _____ *culina*	h) cubicle	_____

For Discussion

Think about private and public spaces in your own house. How do the furnishings and decorations differ in your own private and public spaces?

Projects

1. Using a shoebox (or something similar), construct a model of a Roman *domus* and label all the rooms. Draw in frescoed walls and mosaic floors, and indicate the placement of furniture and the shrine to the household gods.

2. Research how frescoes were painted in Roman times and explain the technique. Find illustrations of Roman frescoes and make a color copy of one, or create your own classically inspired Roman fresco.

3. Research how mosaics were created in Roman times and explain the technique. Find illustrations of Roman mosaics and make a color copy of one, or create your own classically inspired Roman mosaic. (Hint: try using squares cut from construction paper or different types of beans to make your mosaic.)

CHAPTER 5:
DOMESTIC LIFE

FOOD AND MEALS

Fig. 20.
The exterior of a Roman house had little decoration, just a simple doorway, small windows, and an additional security window for the janitor.

Fig. 21.
This *triclinium*, or dining room, is decorated with a brightly colored scene located just behind the base of the left-hand couch from where the guest of honor could best admire it.

As we learned in the last chapter, Romans drew a sharp line between their public and private lives, and extended that division to the layout of the *domus* as well. All but the smallest apartment had some space reserved for receiving guests or clients. In extravagant homes, these spaces were usually large and lavishly decorated, designed to impress and even intimidate a visitor. In humbler dwellings, reception areas mainly served to keep outsiders apart from the private living space of the family.

Although not all Roman houses and apartments had a *triclinium*, a formal dining room, some of the grandest had several. And they could be designated for either public or private use. But whether *triclinia* were indoor or outdoor, lavish or simple, public or private, the basic design was the same. A *triclinium* consisted of three large, three-person couches arranged in a U-shape around a small table. Women, if present at all at a dinner party, normally sat in chairs, at least during the time of the Republic.

Sometimes the couches were permanently installed and sometimes they were movable pieces of furniture. A table, or even several tables, could be placed in the open area in front of the three dining couches. Each couch, from left to right as you faced the room, had a name: *imus* (lowest), *medius* (middle), and *summus* (highest). And the three places for diners to recline on each couch were also called, from left to right, *imus*, *medius*, and *summus*. And so, the person placed in the first position on the first couch on the left was said to be *imus in imo* or the lowest place on the lowest couch. This was the least desirable spot in the room. Since diners reclined on their left side, the person dining *imus in imo* had little opportunity to carry on a conversation during dinner. In fact, this position was so inferior that it was called the *locus libertini* or the freedman's place, since a freedman client, grateful merely to be invited to his patron's house, usually occupied it.

The host traditionally reclined at the highest place on the lowest couch (*summus in imo*). This position enabled him to converse more easily with the guest of honor, who was usually seated at the lowest place on the middle couch (*imus in medio*). This position was referred to as the *locus consularis* or the consul's place, since a person who held the office of *consul* was at the top of the political and social scale. Not surprisingly, Romans paid scrupulous attention to a person's class and rank when assigning places for a banquet in the *triclinium*.

Unfortunately, not enough information survives to inform us where family members were placed when Romans dined privately. Most of our information about dining practices comes from writers who related humorous tales about excessively grand dinner parties. The writer Petronius, for example, tells a story about Trimalchio, a newly wealthy man with little knowledge of customary dining practices, who hosted a party. Trimalchio wrongly but understandably concluded that *summus in summo* (the highest place on the highest couch) must be the best position and therefore took it for himself!

The food served at a formal, three-course meal was often quite sumptuous. But all guests were not necessarily served the same fare. Romans were accustomed to being treated according to their social standing in other areas of life, and dining was no exception. Patrons often differentiated between their guests and served their clients cheaper wine, less expensive meat, and fewer delicacies than their social equals. It was not, however, considered good manners for the host of a dinner party to call attention to the difference in the food served to his guests.

The first course or appetizer (*gustus*) was meant to spur the appetite. It often consisted of eggs, lettuce and other raw vegetables, and/or various shellfish and seafood in sauces. The *cena* was the main course of meats and cooked vegetables, accompanied with wine. Since the appetizer was not considered a true course, the final course, dessert, was called the *secunda mensa* or second table. It included pastries and especially fruits. Thus the expression "from the egg to the apples" (*ab ovo usque ad mala*) describes a complete formal meal from *gustus* to *secunda mensa*. Roman authors, most notably Apicius, recorded many Roman recipes. These recipes, adapted and modified for the modern kitchen, can be found in several excellent cookbooks.

Despite the surviving accounts of extravagant and exotic Roman dining practices, it is quite likely that most Romans ate very simple food and not a great deal of it. The large number of mills and bakeries in Pompeii indicates that bread was rarely baked at home. Of course olives and grapes were plentiful and, when they were processed into oil and wine, could be kept indefinitely. Olive oil was the primary source of dietary fat. Wine, which was stored in concentrated form, was diluted with

American Academy in Rome, Photographic Archive

Fig. 22.
Raw foods, such as the mushrooms shown in this mosaic and vegetables, were served as an appetizer or *gustus*.

water before it was consumed. Preserved, dried, and smoked meat from domesticated animals, game, and seafood were readily available, but lack of refrigeration made these a risky and expensive source of protein. Dormice were a prized delicacy, and these small rodents were bred on farms. Milk from all types of livestock was consumed, but most of the milk was processed into cheese, which had a longer shelf life. Cheeses and legumes were a more common and accessible source of protein than meat.

Garum, a salty and savory sauce made from fermented fish parts, was the condiment of choice and was liberally used in Roman cooking. Since foods such as olive oil, wine, vinegar, grains, cheeses, *garum*, honey, some nuts, and dried legumes and fruits could be stored for relatively long periods of time, the average Roman ate healthily and well even during the winter months. Some foods not available to the ancient Roman were: pasta, oranges, peanuts, potatoes, rice, tomatoes, tea, coffee, butter, and sugar. Honey was used as a sweetener.

Fig. 23.
At a meal in an old-fashioned household, men reclined while women sat in chairs; the food was brought in on small tables.

Romans ate three meals a day. The main meal (*cena*) was usually consumed at midday, although it was sometimes eaten in the evening. The other two meals were light. Breakfast was called *ientaculum* and consisted of bread, perhaps softened with wine or garnished with salt, *garum*, olives, or cheese and washed down with milk, wine or *mulsum*, a beverage consisting of equal parts of wine and honey. If the second light meal of the day was eaten at noon, it was called the *prandium*; if it was consumed in the evening, it was called the *vesperinum*. No matter when it was served, this meal was likely to include cold meats, vegetables, and fruits left over from the previous *cena* or hot food purchased from a *thermopolium* or fast-food vendor. The *cena* was always the largest meal of the day, but the menu for a family meal would not have been as elaborate as one prepared for guests.

MEN'S AND CHILDREN'S CLOTHING

The basic garment of Roman dress was the simple *tunica*, a short sleeved or sleeveless ankle-length shift woven from wool or course fibers such as flax or cheap linen. The *tunica* could be worn in several ways. Usually it was belted and bloused at the waist to about knee length for men. The extra material at the waist could be folded to form a convenient carrying pouch. A sleeveless *tunica* was more comfortable for a person engaged in manual labor. A loincloth called a *subligaculum* was sometimes worn instead of a tunic, but it was not, as a rule, worn as an undergarment. A simple *tunica* and a pair of sandals (*soleae*) or shoes (*calcei*) were sufficient to serve the clothing needs of men, women, children, and slaves for most of the year in the temperate Mediterranean climate. In cold weather, several layers of *tunicae* and leg and arm wrappings were added.

The *toga* was a garment reserved exclusively for citizens. Stripes on both *tunica* and *toga* indicated the rank of the wearer, narrow for a member of the class of *equites* and broad for nobles or patricians. The wealthy, predictably, indulged in more expensive fabrics with finer weaves and more embroidery than the simple, natural colored wool of the garments worn by poorer people. The *toga* was a large, heavy, and cumbersome piece of wool cloth that varied in size, shape, and method of draping through the centuries. Attempts to reconstruct the toga from descriptions or statues yield diverse results.

The *toga* was worn for formal public appearances, civic and religious ceremonies, never in military service, and rarely at home. Togas of Roman men may all look the same to us, but there was as much variety of style and cut through the decades as there is in male business attire in our own day.

Generally, the *toga* was a semicircular seamless piece of wool, elaborately draped over the left shoulder and arm, under the right arm and back over the left shoulder. The draping process was so complicated that a Roman needed the help of another person, usually a slave, to put on a *toga*. Properly draped, tucked, and folded, the *toga* descended to the ankles. A portion of the folded section could be pulled out and drawn over the head for religious ceremonies. Another fold in the front could be used as a pocket.

There were distinctive categories of *togae*, each worn for a different purpose. Children and elected officials wore a *toga* with a border around the edge, called the *toga praetexta*. Symbolically the border protected the person wearing this kind of *toga*. Officials, who safeguarded the State, and children, who were prone to an early death from childhood diseases, needed "protection" that these borders symbolized. When a male child came of age, the ceremony included the dedication of his childhood *toga praetexta* and the celebration of his wearing for the first time the *toga* of a man, *toga virilis* also called the *toga* of a citizen, *toga civilis*, or the plain *toga*, *toga pura*. This was a plain, white *toga*. When a citizen ran for public office, he wore an artificially whitened *toga* called a *toga candida*. The whiteness of his *toga* marked him as a candidate for office.

Sometimes mantles or cloaks of heavy, woven cloth, or even foul weather gear made of leather were fashionable or even practical additions to the *toga*. Hoods and hats, usually broad-brimmed and made of straw or leather, were worn when traveling or in bad weather, not as everyday wear.

Women's Clothing

Roman women, like Roman men, did not wear underwear as we know it. Some women, however, did wear a cloth wound around their chest for support. The *tunica* served as an undergarment or slip that was worn beneath the *stola*, a dress that was open on the sides and pinned at the shoulders with brooches or pins called *fibulae*. The *stola* was bloused at the waist above a belt and extended to cover the ankles.

A Roman woman's outermost garment was a *palla*, a large shawl, wrapped much like a toga and worn only outside the house. The possibilities for variety of fabric, color, and accents of jewelry were abundant, as was the variety of women's hairstyles. A woman's hair was usually long. It was worn simply and close to the scalp or curled or braided in narrow strands and wrapped elaborately in swirls and buns. Often the front of the head was piled high with curls.

Household Hygiene

Only the wealthiest households had private access to running water. But in urban Rome no one was ever far from a public fountain. An abundant supply of safe, clean water was piped into the city via numerous aqueducts or *aquaeductus*.

Fig. 24.
A married woman wore the very modest *palla* and *stola*. Her head is covered in this scene because she is taking part in a religious ritual.

Fig. 25.
These remains of an aqueduct are just outside of Rome.

Romans living in an atrium-style house could collect rainwater channeled from the roof into large receptacles called cisterns. This water was not as safe for drinking, but was fine for washing and cleaning.

Very few houses had indoor toilets with a direct connection to the sewer system. Human waste was gathered from chamber pots and emptied, usually by slaves, into sewage drains in the street. Apartment dwellers were notorious for tossing the contents of chamber pots from their windows or balconies directly into the street. A simple stroll could be hazardous for an inattentive pedestrian.

The city of Rome was well supplied with good water and public latrines and baths. These advances in technology helped to keep the Romans relatively healthy and clean.

HEATING

Although Roman engineers were capable of constructing elaborate central heating systems for the houses and baths of Roman Britain and Germany, few private houses in Italy required them. Seldom were winters uncomfortably cold in the warm Mediterranean climate. Sometimes Romans lit a charcoal brazier to take the chill from individual rooms.

SLEEPING

Roman bedrooms (*cubicula*) were extremely small by our standards. They were used solely for sleeping and were sparsely furnished. Romans did not particularly like to shut themselves away from the rest of the family during the day and felt little need for the kind of privacy many modern people crave. Since artificial lighting was impractical for most activities, Romans did little at night except sleep. They slept on the same kind of couch that was used for dining and sitting during the day. Made of metal, or wood, couches were piled with mattresses and pillows stuffed with feathers or straw.

Chapter 5 Exercises: *Domestic Life*

Word Study

Match each of the following terms with a word associated with it by derivation and explain the connection:

1. _____ *candida*   a) Aquarius   _____

2. _____ *summus*   b) candidate   _____

3. _____ *gustus*   c) summit   _____

4. _____ *thermopolium*   d) textile   _____

5. _____ *medius*   e) thermos   _____

6. _____ *soleae*   f) gustatory   _____

7. _____ *praetexta*   g) median   _____

8. _____ *subligaculum*   h) ligament   _____

9. _____ *aquaeductus*   i) sole   _____

Short Answers

Answer the following questions in the space provided.

1. Besides where they were seated, how else might invited guests at a Roman dinner party be reminded of their status in society?

2. Explain the Latin phrase *ab ovo usque ad mala*.

3. Explain why the dessert course was called *secunda mensa* or second table.

4. What made the consumption of meat risky and expensive?

5. Romans ate three meals a day, only one of which was large. Explain what these three meals were called and whether they were light or heavy meals.

6. What was a shop that sold hot, fast food called?

7. As a rule, did Romans wear underwear?

8. What was the most basic Roman garment, worn by men, women, children, and slaves called?

9. Who wore the following types of togas: *praetexta, virilis* or *civilis, candida*?

10. Name and describe two distinctive garments worn by women.

11. Name two means of obtaining water for household use.

12. How were individual rooms of a Roman house heated?

13. What were Roman beds like?

COULD THEY HAVE EATEN IT?

Decide whether the ingredients of the following items were available to the Romans. Circle the foods that you think the Romans could have eaten.

apple pie	iced tea
pizza	orange marmalade
date and nut bread	fried artichokes
stuffed turkey	pea soup
baked potato	oatmeal
sausage burger on a roll	rice pudding
spaghetti with tomato sauce	egg salad sandwich
bean salad	clams on the half-shell

SMALL GROUP ACTIVITY

Pretend that you and another classmate are a Roman aristocratic couple living during the late Republic in Rome. Your names are L. Cornelius Lentulus and Iulia Minor. You are hosting a dinner party for 12 invited guests: eight men and four women. The names and a brief description of each guest are given below. Decide each person's place on the dining couches in your *triclinium* and the placement of the chairs for the women. Draw an aerial view of the dining room and label each person's place. Explain your choices.

S. Varius Marcellus, a wealthy member of the business class (*equites*), owns many houses in the city, including many in your neighborhood

M. Aurelius Cotta: a former *consul*, recently returned from foreign service in Asia

Valeria: aristocratic wife of M. Aurelius Cotta

Gnaeus Flavius: son of a freedman, legal scholar, former tribune

M. Terentius Epimius: a freedman, an extremely wealthy and successful shoemaker

Astatia: wife of Epimius

M. Cornelius Lentulus: older brother of L. Cornelius Lentulus, a senator

Terentia Prima: wife of L. Cornelius Lentulus

M. Caelius Rufus: a young aristocrat just beginning his political career

P. Ostorius Scapula: an equestrian with distinguished military service

T. Quinctius Flamininus: a patrician currently holding the office of censor

Porcia Maior: wife of T. Quinctius Flamininus

LARGE GROUP PROJECTS

1. Research Roman recipes. Plan and prepare a Roman *cena*.

2. Plan and present a Roman fashion show.

CHAPTER 6: EDUCATION

INTRODUCTION

In ancient Rome it was not the responsibility of the state, but of each family, to educate its children. Aristocrats set the standards and styles for all aspects of Roman life, and education was no exception. The aristocratic method of educating their young became the model for all classes in Roman society.

ELEMENTARY EDUCATION

Almost all boys born into free families, and some girls, received a formal elementary education. Sometimes the *paterfamilias* himself took charge of his children's education. More often, he provided a teacher. The quality of instruction varied enormously, as did the cost. The most expensive option was for the *paterfamilias* to purchase a slave, preferably Greek-speaking, to tutor his children at home. A less expensive alternative was to hire a free man who was a professional teacher or *magister* to give private instruction to the children. The least costly method of providing an education, however, was to send the children to a group school, conducted by the lowest level of teacher, the *magister ludi* (school teacher).

Some families purchased an older slave, known as a *paedagogus*, to accompany the children to school and to protect them from the dangers of the city on the way. The *paedagogus* was expected to carry the children's school books, sit in on their classes to insure that both the students and the teacher were working hard, and assist students with their homework. Many *paedagogi* became such valued family members that they eventually earned their freedom. Once freed, *paedagogi* often turned their years of classroom observation into a career and opened schools of their own.

An elementary education consisted of reading, writing, and simple arithmetic. Students learned the alphabet and how to reproduce and pronounce letters, then syllables, then whole words. Since a *magister* spent most of the time teaching the letters of the alphabet, he was also known as a *litterator*. Schoolchildren practiced writing the alphabet on wax tablets, known as *tabellae*. These were frames made of wood, filled with beeswax, and bound together with leather straps. Students wrote with a *stilus*, a pen-like instrument made of wood, metal, or bone, with a pointed end for scratching the letters into the wax and a flattened, paddle-like end for pressing the wax back for reuse. Simple arithmetic calculations were performed on an *abacus*, a counting board with vertical columns representing amounts in units, tens, and hundreds. Pupils were expected to repeat aloud, both individually and in unison, the teacher's words. As a result, classrooms were very noisy places. Classes were held throughout the city, both outdoors and in the shade of public colonnades.

Since these basic skills were all a child needed to be a productive citizen and, in the case of a boy, a soldier, families with small means and few hopes for their children did not pay for education beyond the elementary level.

GRAMMAR SCHOOL

The next stage was the school of the *grammaticus*, who was usually a slave or a freedman. In this higher level of education, students read and interpreted literature in both Greek and Latin, since well-educated Romans were expected to be bilingual. There was no fixed age for students to complete either their elementary or grammar-school education.

Fig. 26.
In this frieze, a *grammaticus* instructs his pupils in school.

THE *RHETOR*

At the next level of education a student studied under a *rhetor*, a teacher who trained pupils in the art of public speaking. The *rhetor* commanded the highest fees of all types of teachers. Rhetorical training began whenever the *rhetor* agreed to begin instruction, or as soon as the family could afford the expense. The best and costliest *rhetors* were Greeks. Pupils learned to improve their diction and to project their voice.

Rhetoricians encouraged students to prepare speeches that included clever sayings and made reference to well-known characters and situations in literature. Oftentimes students were presented with familiar situations from myth or literature and asked to argue on the side first of one character's actions, then of another's. It was a challenge to create a new and convincing argument. Similarly, students were expected to argue both sides of legal issues.

The final test was to prepare and deliver a *declamatio*, a formal oration performed for the *rhetor*. Once this was successfully accomplished, the student was prepared for the challenges of a public career in the law courts, the army, in political assemblies, and even in the Senate itself.

ADVANCED STUDY

The wealthiest and most gifted young orators occasionally sought additional training abroad in the great centers of Greek learning. There they not only perfected their Greek, but also studied advanced rhetoric, perhaps on the island of Rhodes, or entered one of the great schools of philosophy in Athens. Undoubtedly, some young men did not apply themselves to their studies and wasted their parents' money once they arrived in Greece, but others returned to Rome and used their advanced education to shine as leading politicians, lawyers, and intellectuals of their day.

Chapter 6 Exercises: *Education*

WHO AM I?

Choose the person from the word bank who best fits the descriptions below. Some answers will be used more than once.

rhetor	*paedagogus*	privately hired teacher
grammaticus	privately owned tutor	*magister ludi*

1. Fabius is concerned about the education of his young son Marcus. Marcus is eight years old and is having difficulty reading, even though he has been attending school with six other children for a year. Fabius has decided to withdraw Marcus from school, but he cannot afford to buy an educated Greek slave to tutor Marcus. Who will teach Marcus? _____

2. Sempronia knows that she is a fortunate girl. She is ten years old and, instead of spending her days spinning wool, her father allows her to attend lessons along with her brothers. The children are taught by Aristophantes, her family's Greek slave. Sempronia's favorite activity is learning how to calculate sums on the *abacus*. Who is Aristophantes? _____

3. Quintus and Sextus are not fond of Parmenides. He worries too much. Every morning he wakes them up very early and hurries them off to school. He won't let them take the shortcut to the forum because he says the streets on that route are not safe. The boys tell Parmenides that if he lets them take the shortcut, he will not have to carry their scrolls and *tabellae* so far, but Parmenides won't listen to them. Who is Parmenides? _____

4. Publius is 24 years old. He comes from a long line of politicians. His father, his grandfather, and his great-grandfather were *consuls*. When Publius' grandfather died two months ago, his father delivered a moving funeral oration. Publius admires his father's oratorical ability and plans to ask his father to make arrangements for him to study public speaking in Greece. What kind of teacher is Publius seeking? _____

5. Eudemus asks if he can have a word privately with his master Terentius. When Terentius leads him into the *tablinum*, Eudemus explains that Terentius is not getting his money's worth from the children's teacher. In fact, the teacher frequently arrives late to school. Yesterday, all nine children were waiting under the colonnade for nearly an hour before the teacher appeared. Who is Eudemus? About whom is he complaining? _____

6. Lucius and his sister, Cornelia, both teenagers, are sitting at home in the *peristylium*. Lucius is reciting verses to his sister that his teacher, Hermogenes, has asked him to memorize. Cornelia, who has scrolls of Homer's *Iliad* and Vergil's *Aeneid* in front of her, helps her brother remember the lines. Who is Hermogenes? _____

Word Study

Below are Latin words you have met in this chapter, paired with English words. Establish a connection between the meaning of each Latin word and its English derivative.

1. *grammaticus*   grammar   _____

2. *paedagogus*   pedagogy   _____

3. *tabella*   tablet   _____

4. *stilus*   stylus   _____

5. *rhetor*   rhetorical question   _____

6. *magister*   magisterial   _____

Research

1. Find out how an abacus works. Make one and explain to the class how it was used.

2. Make a *tabella* and demonstrate to the class how it was used.

Chapter 7: Slavery

Introduction

Rome was a slave-owning society. Although the Romans are often portrayed as kind and benevolent in their treatment of slaves, the Roman system of slavery was brutally oppressive and its victims were often subjected to inhuman conditions. But slavery in the Roman world was not racially motivated and it did offer possibilities for emancipation. In those respects, it was fundamentally different from the slavery that existed in America and in the British colonies.

Romans considered neither the concept nor the practice of slavery evil or unusual. They recognized that slavery was contrary to the laws of nature, but accepted it as a law of man. Military victors made slaves of the people they conquered and, as Rome conquered more and more people, slaves began to flood domestic markets. Piracy and kidnapping also increased the supply of slaves.

Fig. 27.
Slaves are at work constructing a building by using a crane on a large wheel.

Slaves were the work force that made many of Rome's greatest achievements possible. Although the Romans seldom acknowledged the importance of their slaves and often lived in fear of slave uprisings, ancient Rome would not have become the mightiest power in the Mediterranean world without slaves.

There is much that remains unknown about slavery in the ancient world. We can only guess at the size of the slave population. We cannot be sure how readily a slave could be distinguished from a free person at sight. Moreover, no literature written by slaves about their experiences survives.

Sources and Markets

Slaves came from many sources. Most were purchased from dealers who acquired their stock from the sale of captives defeated in war or from slave hunters and pirates on the fringes of Roman territories. Slaveholders, who oftentimes had inherited slaves, sold them to raise money. Occasionally slaves were born and bred at home, but this occurred rarely since it was expensive to raise young children until they were old enough to be productive.

Slave dealers held public sales or auctions in slave markets. Typically, slaves were forced to stand on a block, naked, wearing only a metal plaque around their neck listing their age, nationality, and any notable talents or defects. Skilled slaves, such as doctors, teachers, hairdressers, or cooks, not surprisingly, brought higher prices. If a slave's feet had been whitened with chalk, this indicated that the slave was being sold for the first time or had just arrived from outside of Italy.

Types of Slaves

The majority of slaves worked in agriculture and industry. The nature of their work varied enormously. In farming, for example, one slave might perform the lowest type of drudgery, actually pulling a plow through a field, while another was privileged to serve as overseer with power over all the farm slaves. In industry, at one end of the spectrum were slaves who performed the dangerous work of a miner or a quarryman while others produced finely fashioned sculptures or frescoes.

Slaves also served on the staffs of political, religious, and military leaders, as personal attendants, curriers, and secretaries. The navy depended on slaves as oarsmen. Forced to endure difficult and dangerous conditions, galley slaves who rowed below decks were crucial to the success of the Roman navy. Public slaves were the property of the government and kept the city in good working order. They cleaned and repaired the streets, sewers, buildings, bridges, and aqueducts.

American Academy in Rome, Photographic Archive

Fig. 28.
Three household slaves groom their mistress and arrange her hair.

Household slaves were usually the most fortunate. Of course they performed many lowly and disagreeable tasks, but some positions entailed considerable responsibility and commanded respect. Traditionally, household slaves served as nursemaids, tutors and bodyguards to school-age children, doormen, dressers, cooks, and secretaries. Larger households required several types of secretaries, for example, those in charge of correspondence, finances, and record keeping.

While many slaves, constantly in fear of brutal punishment, led a wretched life of relentless toil, others, usually the trained and educated, attained privileged positions and were well-treated members of their household. Indeed, some of the luckier slaves probably ate and dressed better than many of the poor residents of the same neighborhood. Despite this, the devastating effect of the loss of personal freedom cannot be underestimated.

Some Legal Aspects of Slavery

Legally, slaves, like animals, were property. As such, they could be bought, sold, given away, or killed at the whim of their owners. Slaveholders exercised complete control over their slaves and could punish misbehavers severely. Runaway slaves were legally guilty of theft; they had stolen themselves.

PUNISHMENTS AND REWARDS

The fear of punishment was an effective way to keep slaves under control. Corporal punishment was common, and slaves were whipped, beaten, branded, and mutilated. Punishment was customarily exacted with other slaves present to terrorize the onlookers into obedience. Although harsh and excessive cruelty towards slaves was socially unacceptable and often criticized by Romans themselves, the practice continued.

Runaway slaves were a constant problem. Upon their capture and return, offenders were often branded or fitted with permanent metal collars identifying them as fugitives. A particularly troublesome slave might be sold to the galleys, the mines, or to a gladiatorial school where their prospects for survival were bleak at best. A slave who made an attempt on the life of a master or participated in an insurrection received the most gruesome punishment - crucifixion. Hanging on a wooden cross brought about a slow and agonizing death by asphyxiation as the lungs of the victim gradually collapsed. If a slaveholder was murdered and the murderer was not found, it was not uncommon for all the slaves in the household to be put to death.

American Academy in Rome, Photographic Archive

Fig. 29.
This non-removable slave collar states that the slave wearing it should be returned to his master for a reward.

To encourage cooperative behavior, slaveholders customarily allowed slaves to receive and keep a small amount of money as savings toward the eventual purchase of their freedom (or to buy a slave of their own). Owners could, if they chose, recognize marriage between slaves. These "rewards" might appear to be acts of kindness or generosity on the part of the owner. Actually, they were an effective way to control the behavior of slaves as an alternative to punishment.

MANUMISSION

Manumission was the legal process by which a slave acquired freedom. A freed slave was awarded a felt cap or bonnet, called a *pilleus*, as a symbol of his newly gained freedom.

Many owners freed slaves in their wills. This, however, was not always an act of kindness. It was, indeed, more economical to free older slaves than to maintain them when they were no longer productive. And furthermore, freeing slaves in a will was a mark of status, a visible sign of the wealth of the deceased.

Slaves not freed in wills could be granted their freedom for various reasons. Some were rewarded for their service or talent; others simply grew too old to be productive. Slaves sometimes purchased their own freedom from their savings, usually at a price agreed upon well in advance. Customarily the cost of freedom was the purchase price of a younger replacement. Slaves were also allowed to purchase the freedom of their family members.

The Romans differed from almost every other slave-owning society in the frequency and regularity with which they freed their slaves. Once formally freed, ex-slaves were eligible for Roman citizenship and the process of assimilation into the class structure of Roman society.

SATURNALIA

The most joyous holiday of the Roman year was the festival of the Saturnalia, a celebration in honor of the god Saturn that began on December 17. Festivities lasted for about seven days and included the exchanging of wax candles and small gifts, such as clay figurines. Merry-making, feasting, and the reversal of the social order marked the Saturnalia. Slaves dined before their masters and discipline was lax. Citizens abandoned the toga in favor of more casual clothing and even wore the *pilleus*, the cap traditionally associated with freed slaves. With good reason the Saturnalia was the holiday most eagerly anticipated by Roman slaves.

Chapter 7 Exercises: *Slavery*

TRUE OR FALSE

Indicate whether each statement is true or false. If it is false, identify the error and correct it.

1. _____ It was easy to spot slaves on the streets of Rome.

2. _____ Most of what we know about the life of a slave comes from surviving autobiographies of slaves.

3. _____ Most of the slaves in ancient Rome were captives taken in war.

4. _____ Slaves were sold at a fixed rate, regardless of their background or special skills.

5. _____ A red mark on the forehead of a slave sold at auction indicated that he or she was being sold for the first time.

6. _____ Much of the city maintenance work was performed by public slaves.

7. _____ Legally, slaves were no different from animals and could be bought, sold, or given away at the whim of their owners.

8. _____ Whipping and branding were the most serious punishments that a slave could be forced to endure.

9. _____ Roman slaves were not permitted to have or use money.

10. _____ A *pilleus* was a cap and a symbol of freedom awarded to a freed slave.

11. _____ It was a mark of status for a master to free his slaves in his will.

12. _____ Ex-slaves and their descendants were not eligible for Roman citizenship.

13. _____ During the celebration of the Saturnalia, masters tended to relax the disciplinary measures they normally exercised over their slaves.

SHORT ANSWERS

Answer the following questions in the space provided.

1. Briefly explain two ways that slavery in ancient Rome differed from slavery in America or in the British Colonies.

2. What were two of the sources of slaves in ancient Rome?

3. Name some of the special duties and responsibilities of house slaves.

4. Why was it relatively unusual for a slave to be born and bred at home?

5. How did a potential buyer learn about the skills of a slave who was being auctioned for sale in the market?

6. Give examples of high-level and low-level tasks performed by slaves in the areas of agriculture and industry.

7. Why were slaves often forced to witness the brutal treatment of their fellow slaves?

8. How might a fugitive slave who had been recaptured be recognized by others?

9. What were some of the alternatives to punishment that masters used to ensure cooperative behavior among their slaves?

10. Why would a master allow a slave to purchase his or her own freedom?

11. Explain why a master would free slaves in his will.

12. What effect might the ability eventually to become a Roman citizen have had on the slave?

GROUP ACTIVITIES

1. Plan a Saturnalia banquet in your classroom.

2. Explain the connection between the French cap of liberty worn at the end of the 18th century by the French people during the French Revolution and the Roman *pilleus.* What historical events occurred in 18th –century France that made the symbol of the cap of liberty appropriate?

3. Write an imaginary slave's autobiography. Include where and when the slave was born and how he or she was acquired as a slave. Describe the slave's owner and the type of work he or she performs. Also mention the slave's reaction to slavery and hopes for the future.

4. Make a placard for the slave whose autobiography you have invented.

CHAPTER 8: FREEDMEN AND FREEDWOMEN

LIBERTINI VS. *LIBERTI*

A slave could gain freedom in many different ways, and some methods of manumission conferred a higher status on the freed slave than others. Only those slaves who were properly and legally freed were officially known as *libertini* or "freedpeople." A legally freed man was called a *libertinus*, and a legally freed woman was called a *libertina*.

An ex-slave who became legally free was eligible for Roman citizenship. But even when a slave became a citizen, the bond between former slave and former master did not end. The master now became a patron and the slave his client. This new relationship was different and more complex than the patron's relationship with his other clients. And there was a special word to signal this special bond. A male ex-slave was known as the *libertus*, a female ex-slave the *liberta* of their former master, but the term was used only when referring a former slave's bond to his or her former master. If, for example, one referred to M. Tullius Tiro as a *libertus* of Cicero, that meant that Tiro was a former slave and now a client of his former master, M. Tullius Cicero. The word *libertinus* described the slave's legal status, whereas the word *libertus* indicated his social status.

Fig. 30.
A funerary inscription for the freedman Gaius Julius Hermes, who lived 34 years, 5 months and 14 days.

PATRON AND CLIENT

How was the nature of the relationship between the patron and his *liberti* different from that between the patron and his other clients? *Liberti* were considered lifetime members of their *familia* and, as such, they were expected to act accordingly. Their patron, in a sense, continued to be their *paterfamilias*. In addition to the services and support required of any client by his patron, *liberti* were expected to obey without question their former owners and to treat them with the same devotion that Roman children in a *familia* owed their parents. Consequently, ex-slaves continued to perform small tasks, without reimbursement, for their patrons, both voluntarily and at their patron's bidding. And just as Roman children were not permitted to take legal action against their parents, so ex-slaves were not permitted to sue their former owners for any reason.

Liberti would, of course, support their patron in politics and vote on public matters as their patron wished, although the voting power of *libertini* as a group did not carry so much political weight as the voting power of the higher classes. And what could *liberti* hope to receive from their patron in return?

Newly freed slaves were in great need of the protection, advice, and financial support that a good patron was expected to provide. For the remainder of this chapter we will discuss situations which applied to all *libertini* in general.

RIGHTS AND RESTRICTIONS OF *LIBERTINI*

Libertini were allowed to own and to transfer property, including slaves. They could make wills and press charges in court. They could marry a member of any class except the senatorial class. In short, they enjoyed nearly all the personal rights of a freeborn Roman citizen. Furthermore, some opportunities were reserved strictly for *libertini*. Only *libertini*, for example, were hired as urban firemen. And some religious offices, usually in outlying towns, could be held only by *libertini*.

Libertini, on the other hand, were excluded from many pursuits that were considered "honorable." They were not permitted, for example, to seek any of the higher political offices, those in the *cursus honorum*. This privilege, however, was open to their sons and their descendants, all of whom were considered full-fledged Roman citizens. Furthermore, *libertini* were not permitted to serve on a major jury or to join the army as legionary soldiers. (Most were already too old to join by the time they were freed.)

OCCUPATIONS

Although *libertini* were employed in almost every occupation except politics and the military, they frequently practiced whatever trade they had learned as a slave. Their patron often provided the financial assistance necessary for them to establish their own business. Since they had everything to gain, they often took on jobs considered less desirable by the Romans, such as dry-cleaning, acting, and banking or money lending. In the early days of the Empire, *libertini* performed most of the bureaucratic jobs, especially as accountants and record keepers. Evidence from inscriptions shows that some *libertinae*, or freedwomen, were astute businesswomen. They kept shops and practiced such professions as midwifery (assisting with births), sewing, and weaving.

Fig. 31.
An actor, wearing a mask, rests against a column.

Fig. 32.
A midwife and her assistant help to deliver a baby. Roman women gave birth in a birthing chair.

ATTITUDES TOWARD *LIBERTINI*

Romans, as we have seen, lived in a class-conscious society, and *libertini* were near the bottom. In spite of their newly acquired status as citizens and the legal protection this afforded them, *libertini* endured many forms of social prejudice. Those who worked hard and earned enough money to insure a comfortable life for themselves and for their children were often looked down upon by more established citizens as greedy opportunists.

American Academy in Rome, Photographic Archive

Fig. 33.
A butcher, possibly a freedman, is hard at work.

Why did the Romans willingly grant freedom and the right of citizenship to so many former slaves? Surely many slaves were manumitted because of a genuine sense of gratitude or affection on the part of their owners, or as a reward for exceptional service, or even as an incentive to ensure the cooperation of other slaves.

The practice of granting freedom may also stem from the fact that most of Rome's earliest slaves were local people, prisoners of wars fought within the confines of the Italian peninsula. Once freed, they were likely to maintain a strong connection to Rome, even if they returned home. Granting freedom was a way to encourage peaceful support for Rome throughout the Italian peninsula and abroad.

Perhaps the Romans never truly believed that birth was as important to the process of being a Roman as was education and societal conditioning. Indeed, as a result of their own mixed origins, Romans believed that, with proper training, anyone could become a Roman.

Chapter 8 Exercises: *Freedmen and Freedwomen*

TRUE OR FALSE

Indicate whether each statement is true or false. If it is false, identify the error and correct it.

1. _____ A slave could gain freedom in many different ways, and some methods of manumission conferred a higher status on the freed slave than others.

2. _____ After slaves gained legal freedom, they normally chose to sever all ties with their former master.

3. _____ Clients, even those who had once been the slaves of their patron, all enjoyed the same relationship with their patron.

4. _____ Slaves who attained their freedom often sued their former masters in court for the abuse they had suffered.

5. _____ The voting power of *libertini* as a group carried just as much political weight as the voting power of the other classes.

6. _____ *Libertini* were not allowed to own property or slaves, nor could they press charges in court.

7. _____ *Libertini* could marry a member of any social class.

8. _____ *Libertini* were not permitted to seek any offices in the *cursus honorum*, although this privilege was open to their sons and their descendants.

9. _____ *Libertini* usually practiced whatever trade they had learned as slaves.

10. _____ Freedwomen were not permitted to work in business or to have a profession.

11. _____ Granting freedom was a way to encourage peaceful support for Rome at home and abroad.

12. _____ Once *libertini* gained citizenship, they blended comfortably and without prejudice into all spheres of Roman society.

SHORT ANSWERS

Answer the following questions in the space provided.

1. Explain the meaning of the words *libertini* and *liberti*.

2. List some of the rights and restrictions of *libertini*.

3. What sort of obligations did *liberti* have to their former master?

4. Why would a freed slave want to maintain a relationship with his former master?

5. Give some reasons why the Romans granted freedom and the right of citizenship so frequently to slaves.

6. Comment on the attitudes of Romans of different social classes toward freedpeople.

WHO AM I?

Decide whether the person described below is a

libertinus/libertina	*libertus/liberta*
descendant of a *libertinus/libertina*	slave

1. Because I am a strong man, I must pull heavy farm equipment all day long. I live in fear of physical punishment. _____

2. When I was a young man, my master trained me to bake; now every morning I wait for him in his *atrium* with fine loaves of bread from my bakery. _____

3. Tomorrow I will marry Marcus Cornelius Rufus, a distinguished senator. My father, considering his background, is understandably pleased. _____

4. I remember vividly the day I assisted my mistress when she gave birth to her daughter Flavia. I could barely speak Latin then. Now I earn my living as a midwife, assisting women in the delivery of their children. _____

5. I would rather work hard and endure this humiliation than risk escape to my native country. I keep reminding myself that my present condition is temporary and my children can have a fine life here. _____

FOR DISCUSSION

Imagine that you are a middle-aged man or woman who has been a slave for most of your life. Your master, who is a distinguished Roman senator, has just freed you. What choices will you make and how will your life change immediately and in the future?

WRITING ASSIGNMENT

Create an autobiography of a freedman or a freedwoman.

CHAPTER 9:
URBAN LIFE

INTRODUCTION

Rome was one of the largest cities in the ancient world. Toward the end of the Republic about one million people inhabited the city. This number rose to nearly two million two centuries later. If population estimates are correct, the city of Rome at this time had roughly the same size and density as Houston, Texas, the fourth-largest city in the United States. Although the residents of Rome often complained about crowded conditions, the population density was far less than that of modern Hong Kong, Calcutta, or even New York.

AREAS OF THE CITY

Rome is situated inland at a bend of the Tiber River, which flows into the Mediterranean Sea at Ostia, Rome's seaport. Rome's seven distinctive hills resembled ridges or volcanic fingers that stretched, like a seven-fingered hand, through the city. The names of the hills are the Capitoline, Palatine, Aventine, Esquiline, Quirinal, Caelian, and Viminal. Between the Palatine and the Capitoline was a dank and unhealthy marsh. Shortly after the founding of the city, during the Monarchy, the Romans built a drainage system called the *Cloaca Maxima* that channeled this low-lying water into the Tiber. Between the Capitoline and the Palatine the Romans developed the reclaimed land into an area that became known as the *Forum Romanum* or the Roman Forum.

The word *forum* is related the Latin word *foris*, which means "outdoors." And the *Forum* was just that: a place outdoors. Filled with temples, shrines, and public buildings, the *Forum* was the religious, political, and social center of the city. It was "downtown" Rome. The nearby area flanking the Tiber teemed with warehouses, markets, and shops. Rome was a thriving metropolis.

Fig. 34.
A view of the Forum with the Temple of Saturn in the foreground, the Temple of Antoninus Pius and Faustina in the back, left and the Temple of Castor and Pollux in the back, right.

The hills, offering fresher, cooler air, attractive views, and a retreat from the noise and commotion of the city below, were the most desirable places to live. The Palatine, with its view of both the *Forum* and, later, the *Circus Maximus*, was the most fashionable hill. It became the neighborhood of choice for the rich and famous, who rivaled each other in the splendor of their homes. In fact, our word "palace" is derived from the name of the Palatine hill.

By contrast, an area known as the *Subura*, towards the foot of the Viminal, was generally an unpleasant, unsafe, overcrowded neighborhood with many dilapidated *insulae*. But the rich and the poor of Rome lived in an integrated society, especially on hills like the Esquiline and in the upper reaches of some of the valleys. Julius Caesar, for example, who came from a wealthy patrician family, was born in the *Subura*. Similarly, not all the houses on the Palatine were palatial.

Large public and private gardens and parks, both in the center and on the outskirts of the city, provided much-needed green space and sunlit areas. On a casual walk through the city an ancient pedestrian might pass through narrow and dark residential streets, noisy and busy commercial areas, dazzling and majestic public spaces, and winding paths through parks and gardens.

The average Roman walked everywhere in the city. Wealthy men and women, however, often preferred to be transported in vehicles carried on the shoulders of slaves. One type of vehicle was a *sella* or sedan chair, another was a *lectica*, an enclosed cubicle containing a couch. If a Roman did not own his own *sella* or *lectica*, he could hire one, much as people today call a cab or hire a limousine. These ancient vehicles solved a serious transportation problem for those who did not care to walk through the city. To alleviate traffic, wheeled vehicles were prohibited by law in the city during working hours, but neither a *sella* nor a *lectica* had wheels. Because of this law, all deliveries that required the use of carts and wagons took place at night. Many Romans complained about the constant noise in the city.

Roads and Buildings

Streets were another example of the engineering skill of the Romans. Paved with large, smooth, closely fitted black paving stones, they were slightly crowned to permit water to run off into sewer openings on the sides. At intervals, three stones were sometimes set horizontally into the pavement of the street itself.

Fig. 35.
Roman city streets, like this one in Pompeii, were frequently filled with water and debris.

These served two purposes: they provided a way for pedestrians to cross a muddy or flooded street comfortably and, much like our speed bumps, they slowed down traffic.

There were no effective defensive gates or city walls around the entire city from shortly after 200 BCE to 271 CE. On the periphery of this sprawling city was a dense maze of narrow, winding streets lined with buildings two to eight stories high. Sometimes structures were so tall and streets were so narrow that sunlight rarely penetrated the musty gloom.

Buildings in residential areas were made of brick with a wooden roof topped with terra cotta tiles. The façade was often covered with a layer of stucco, a plaster-like substance that was usually painted, either in a single color or with multi-colored designs. Instead of stucco, grander buildings, closer to the city's center, were often faced with a thin veneer of travertine, a local grayish white marble, or even with more exotically colored imported marble.

Owners of residential buildings, such as *insulae* (apartment houses) or *domus* (single family dwellings), leased space on the first floor, facing the street, to merchants and tradesmen of all varieties. When *tabernae* or shops were open for business, merchandise often spilled out onto the sidewalks and into the streets. The exterior walls of *tabernae* were frequently covered with graffiti. Typically, Roman graffiti consisted of notices about public games, election slogans, or simply personal remarks, good and bad, about people. Water fountains at crossroads offered to city dwellers an abundant supply of fresh, clean water from Rome's many aqueducts. Also at crossroads were neighborhood shrines dedicated to favorite gods or goddesses.

As one neared the *Forum Romanum*, large public buildings and monuments loomed into view. These included impressive temples, the Senate House or *Curia*, and *basilicae*, enormous rectangular buildings with a center aisle and smaller side aisles. *Basilicae* were utilitarian structures that served various functions. One *basilica* in the Forum, the Basilica Aemelia, was a commercial center where individual merchants sold their wares in stalls set up

Fig. 36.
This aqueduct in Turkey, serving the city of Priene, shows how aqueducts moved water through hills and over valleys.

between the internal colonnades; another, the Basilica Julia, served as a legal center and housed law courts. Between the two *basilicae* was the *Rostra*, a large, open-air stage where noted Romans delivered public speeches and orations or where judges conducted high-profile legal trials that were sure to draw large crowds of spectators.

Fig. 37.
On the Arch of Titus, one of the monuments in the Forum, are inscribed the words SENATVS POPVLVSQVE ROMANVS, often abbreviated SPQR.

A little farther beyond the *Rostra*, near the imposing Temple of Castor and Pollux, was a slave market. During the business day the Forum buzzed with activity and was crowded with Romans of all social strata as well as slaves and foreigners.

Towering above all the hustle and bustle of the Forum, on the summit of the Capitoline, were grand and stately temples and the *Tabularium*, the building where public records were kept. And not far away was the *Campus Martius*, a broad, flat area dedicated to Mars, the god of war, where generals trained their soldiers. In this region of Rome were bath complexes, theaters, stadiums, and assembly and voting areas.

Along the left bank of the Tiber was another forum called the *Forum Boarium*, where cattle were bought and sold. Nearby were huge warehouses, granaries, and docks.

THE PUBLIC WATER SUPPLY

Since the Tiber, a muddy and polluted river, was not a practical source of clean drinking water, the Romans built massive aqueducts (*aquaeductus*) that channeled water into Rome from clean springs and rivers in the surrounding hills and mountains. Some aqueducts supplied water from as far as 60 miles away.

Aqueducts channeled water into the city in pipes and trenches whose downward slope was carefully calculated to assist the natural force of gravity. The channels and reservoirs or settling tanks were scrupulously maintained and cleaned to prevent pollution and to inhibit the growth of harmful bacteria. An abundant supply of water gushed continually from public fountains. The overflow spilled directly into the street and then into the sewer system, providing a constant flow of water back into the Tiber.

Although some *domus* and *insulae* had pipes that connected them directly to the aqueducts and to the *Cloaca Maxima*, enabling them to have their own latrines, most city dwellers relied on public facilities or used chamber pots. Whether the contents of chamber pots were emptied into the sewer or dumped into the street, one way or another they were absorbed into the active sewers of Rome.

Fig. 38.
Aqueducts like this one supplied the city with clean water for drinking and bathing.

Fig. 39.
At the very end of the constantly flowing aqueducts were basins, the main source of water for the people of the neighborhood and for the sewer under the street.

Numerous *latrinae* or public bathrooms were conveniently located throughout the city, some of which were attractively decorated. Typically, they consisted of a bench of seats set over a channel of constantly flowing water. A smaller channel in front was used to rinse off the communal sponges-on-sticks that served as toilet paper. There were no cubicles for privacy. Each person's ample clothing fostered some degree of modesty.

American Academy in Rome, Photographic Archive

Fig. 40.
This *latrina* or public bathroom has seats placed over a water channel. Another channel in front of the bench was used for cleaning the public sponge-on-a-stick which served as toilet paper.

Laundries needed not only water to fill their washing and rinsing tanks, but urine. Urine turns into an ammonia-like liquid that was used as a cleaning agent. To ensure that their shops had enough urine for washing clothes, fullers set out large clay pots near their doorways and encouraged male passersby to urinate into them. As unpleasant as it may seem, this practice assisted in the removal of human waste.

Fig. 41.
This is the main pool of the bathing complex of the hot springs spa, *Aquae Sulis*, in Bath, England.

Fig. 42.
Note the large wash basin in one of the bath complexes in Pompeii.

The sophisticated water system also made possible public baths, known as *balneae* or *thermae*. Roman baths, which could be large complexes or small-scale operations, were not only places to bathe, but served as social, athletic, and even intellectual and cultural centers as well. People frequented their favorite bathhouses and met their friends there, much as people today spend time in a gym or a health club. Baths generally had an exercise area called a *palaestra.* Here visitors exercised with weights, played with balls, or engaged in wrestling matches. They could also enjoy massages and have their body hair plucked. Some of the larger and better-equipped bath complexes housed libraries and displayed important works of sculpture and painting for the cultural enjoyment of their clientele.

Baths had rooms containing pools of different temperatures: the *frigidarium* or cold room, the *tepidarium* or warm room, and the *caldarium* or hot room. Water was heated by an elaborate system of furnaces below called the *hypocaustum.* Slaves stoked the wood-burning furnaces that channeled warm air under the floor and through the walls, heating both the rooms and the bathing pools in them. Thus the Romans had many opportunities to exercise and attend to their personal grooming and hygiene.

ILLNESS AND CONTAGION

Despite good food, plenty of water, effective sewage management, and a culture that encouraged frequent bathing and regular exercise, Romans, of course, did contract illnesses. At times, uncontrollable plagues ravished the population. There were no hospitals in Rome until the fourth century. Doctors were mostly Greek slaves or freedmen who were neither highly regarded for their medical skill nor trusted. Herbal medicines and potions of all kinds were prescribed, but scientific cures were, for the most part, unknown. Sickness often resulted in death.

Romans paid scrupulous attention to the disposal of their dead. Inhumation, or burial in the ground of an intact corpse, was absolutely prohibited inside the city, thus diminishing the spread of contagion. More commonly, bodies were cremated, and this, too, took place far away from populated zones.

PERILS OF THE CITY

Despite successful measures to make Rome a safe and pleasant place to live, urban life could be perilous. Some *insulae* were dangerously overcrowded and poorly ventilated. Sometimes buildings collapsed from shoddy construction and disrepair. Whole neighborhoods were destroyed by the frequent fires that spread through the city. Crime was another problem. Petty thievery and mob violence occurred regularly. But despite these problems, Rome was one of the best managed and culturally stimulating cities in the ancient Mediterranean world.

Chapter 9 Exercises: *Urban Life*

WORD SEARCH

Find the names of the seven hills of Rome.

```
P   A   Q   U   I   R   I   N   A   L   S   E
A   D   V   U   Z   A   V   R   T   O   A   S
L   I   E   E   L   P   A   L   S   A   C   Q
A   J   Q   L   N   A   E   L   I   V   A   U
T   C   A   P   I   T   O   L   I   N   E   I
I   I   E   S   Q   O   I   R   I   N   L   L
N   I   N   V   I   M   I   N   A   L   I   I
E   C   M   E   U   P   L   I   E   A   A   N
S   O   S   Q   T   V   N   A   L   C   N   E
```

FILL IN THE BLANKS

Use the following word bank to fill in the blanks.

fountains	*thermae*	*tepidarium*	*caldarium*	*hypocaustum*
latrinae	Ostia	Palatine	*Forum Romanum*	clean water
Cloaca Maxima	Tiber	Capitoline	aqueducts	*frigidarium*
balneae				

Water and the City of Rome

1. One of the earliest engineering feats of the Romans was the construction of the
_____, the city's sewer system. By using it to drain the marsh that lay in
the valley between the _____ and the _____ hills, the Romans
were able to make use of the land that eventually became the _____.

2. The _____ flows through the city of Rome and empties into the sea at
_____, Rome's seaport. It was here that most of the city's importing and
exporting of trade goods took place. Smaller vessels, however, could sail on to Rome
where they loaded and unloaded their cargo at docks and warehouses on the river bank.

3. Although the river was an important commercial waterway, it was not a source of _____. To provide the city with the water it needed, the Romans constructed an elaborate system of _____, which were carefully maintained.

4. Some residences in the city had their own water supply, but most people obtained their water from public _____, commonly located at crossroads.

5. Public toilets, called _____, were conveniently located throughout the city. Waste matter was flushed away into the sewer.

6. One of the triumphs of the Romans' ability to manage water was the abundance of bathhouses and bathing complexes throughout the city. Called _____ or _____, baths offered the opportunity for bathers to submerge themselves into a cold pool called a _____, a warm pool, called a _____, or a hot pool, called a _____. The regulation of water temperature was controlled by a slave-powered heating system called a _____.

MATCHING COLUMNS

Match each of the buildings or places in the first column with the correct identification in the second column.

1. _____ *Tabularium*   a) by definition, a place outdoors

2. _____ *Curia*   b) speaker's platform

3. _____ *Subura*   c) single-family dwelling

4. _____ *taberna*   d) cattle market

5. _____ forum   e) Senate House

6. _____ *Campus Martius*   f) army's training ground

7. _____ *domus*   g) crowded and densely populated area

8. _____ Rostra   h) a desirable place to live

9. _____ Palatine   i) large, rectangular building

10. _____ *insula*   j) shop

11. _____ *Forum Boarium*   k) apartment house

12. _____ *basilica*   l) repository for public records

13. _____ *palaestra*   m) an exercise area in a bathhouse

FOR DISCUSSION

Discuss the pros and cons of life in the city for an ancient Roman of average means.

CHAPTER 10:
LAW AND ORDER

INTRODUCTION

Rome, like any large, overcrowded city today, could be a dangerous place to live. Predictably, crime, violence, and fire were three of the greatest hazards of urban life. In this chapter we will examine how the Romans reacted to, coped with, and tried to remedy these problems over the course of time.

ADDRESSING CRIME, VIOLENCE, AND FIRE IN THE REPUBLIC

In the early days of the Republic, citizens of Rome and of the smaller outlying towns and villages, for the most part, protected each other. In such a small, homogenous community environment, neighbors worked together to combat and eliminate crime, violence, and destruction caused by fire. As the population increased, inhabitants no longer knew or trusted their neighbors and the effectiveness of self-protection in crowded neighborhoods decreased.

In theory, the two consuls and the urban praetor, the highest elected officials in Rome, had the legal right and power to arrest, prosecute, and punish the perpetrator of any crime committed in violation of Roman law. In practice, however, these officials had no ready means to apprehend alleged criminals. There was no police force in ancient Rome. Aediles were minor elected officials just starting out on their political careers and their primary responsibility was to keep the city in good, safe running order, especially when it came to public areas such as markets and streets. They appear to have been better equipped to apprehend and prosecute those who threatened the safety of the city. If the interpretation of surviving records is correct, aediles worked closely with a board of three men who had at their disposal a group of several hundred public slaves. This force of slaves was used to apprehend, incarcerate, and punish evildoers, and even, to a lesser extent, to fight fires and to patrol the streets at night. Unfortunately, little is known about their specific responsibilities, organization, and activities. Furthermore. their small numbers must have prevented them from functioning as an effective means to combat crime and danger throughout the city. How could a crowded city like Rome manage without a police and a fire department?

THE CASE AGAINST A POLICE DEPARTMENT

Strange as it may seem, the ruling elite of Republican Rome did not want or need a police force. Wealthy patrons could rely on their large retinue of clients to protect them whenever they ventured outside. As we have seen, their houses were quite secure and were staffed with enough slaves to insure reliable protection against burglars or fires during the day or night. If they wanted more personal protection, these Romans had the financial means to hire private bodyguards. And so, the wealthiest and most influential Romans were relatively safe from urban perils.

Of greater concern to the upper classes and to the Senate than fear of civil crime and violence was the possibility that rival political factions, aided by an armed police force, might seize power by violent means. And so, during the Republic, an effort was made to keep armed troops outside the city and a police force was never instituted.

Addressing Crime, Violence, and Fire in the Empire

Augustus, the first emperor of Rome, began to address the problem of safety in the city seriously. Although most of the measures that he instituted were designed to insure his own personal safety, he also hoped to keep the city free from the dangers of crime, violence (especially that caused by social unrest), and fire. To accomplish this, he developed three military units: the Praetorian Guard (*Praetoriani*), the Urban Cohorts (*Urbanici*), and the Watchmen (*Vigiles*).

The Praetorian Guard was entrusted with the responsibility of protecting and guarding the emperor himself. The guard was made up of elite soldiers and centurions from the legions. They lived in a camp just outside the city walls. Although they did not have any specific civic duties, they could be called upon in time of crisis to help maintain order. In fact, their presence alone was a deterrent to rioting and protests. Later emperors did not hesitate to use the Praetorian Guard to crush dissent and uprisings. As time passed, the leaders of the Praetorian Guard, known as prefects (*praefecti*), became more and more powerful. Several times in the course of Roman history the Praetorian Guard assassinated emperors and created new ones.

American Academy in Rome, Photographic Archive

Fig. 43.
Members of the Praetorian Guard listen to a speech by the Emperor.

The Urban Cohorts were as close to a police force as we can find in the ancient world. Its leader, the Urban Prefect, was entrusted with the task of maintaining order and gaining intelligence. In all probability, they were housed in the same camp as the Praetorian Guard. The Urban Cohorts patrolled the city during the day but, unfortunately, we know very little about their responsibilities and activities.

The last of these units were the Watchmen. The primary function of the Watchmen or *Vigiles* was to fight fires. The *Vigiles* themselves were *libertini*, or legally freed slaves, but their leaders were centurions and tribunes from the regular army. *Vigiles* did not live with the Praetorian and Urban Guard, but were housed in seven separate stations spread equally among the fourteen regions of the city. Their barracks were located near the boundary between their two regions, close to the city walls, and always on a major access road leading to the center of Rome. They also had substations, from which they patrolled the city by night in small groups. The principal task of the *Vigiles* was to spot and suppress small fires before they raged out of control. If a fire in their regions became a dangerous threat, they could summon additional men and equipment from the stations in other regions of the city.

Vigiles smothered fires with blankets and doused them with buckets of water, sand or vinegar. They carried pikes and axes to dismantle a burning structure and blankets, ropes, and ladders to help in rescue efforts. They wore helmets for protection but carried no armor or weapons. As night watchmen, they responded to any crimes or cries for help they encountered. Although they were an important force in the maintenance of law and order, their primary function was to protect Rome from fire.

APPREHENDING CRIMINALS

Some of the offenses that are treated as criminal offenses today were tried in civil courts in ancient Rome. Victims of theft, property damage, assault, and slander, for example, were themselves responsible for bringing the offenders into civil court in order to sue them for damages. Crimes against the state, on the other hand, included attempts at conspiracy, participation in civil disturbances or riots, and membership in certain political or religious groups. In such cases an effort was made by the state to apprehend the perpetrators.

A wrongdoer in Rome could be apprehended by any of the anti-crime units, or by private citizens, depending on the nature of the offense. If the crime threatened the emperor, the Praetorian Guard was expected to apprehend the criminal. If the crime threatened public safety, the Urban Cohorts made the arrest. Perpetrators of civil crimes were apprehended by private citizens or by the *Vigiles*.

SENTENCING AND PUNISHMENT

Any of the prefects or aediles had the right to arrest, detain, and even brutally beat an evildoer. Cases involving more serious crimes required a praetor who had the authority to inflict capital punishment on the tried and convicted offender. A free citizen condemned to death was strangled, beheaded, or, in the case of lower class offenders, worked to death in the mines, in ships' galleys, or forced to face wild beasts in the arena. The more fortunate offenders were sent to gladiatorial schools, where there was at least a chance for survival and freedom. A slave convicted of a capital crime was typically sentenced to crucifixion.

The system that evolved for maintaining law, order, and safety in ancient Rome was certainly not without its faults. It did, however, make Rome safer from fire and more secure from crime than almost any other large cosmopolitan center in the ancient world.

Chapter 10 Exercises: *Law and Order*

True or False

Indicate whether each statement is true or false. If it is false, identify the error and correct it.

1. _____ Crime, violence, and fire are still three of the greatest hazards of urban life.

2. _____ As population increases the effectiveness of self-protection in crowded neighborhoods tends to decrease.

3. _____ The two consuls and the urban praetor had men at their disposal to apprehend criminals.

4. _____ The wealthy citizens of Rome were the people most likely to be victimized by crime and violence in the city.

5. _____ During the Republic, the upper classes were in favor of having armed men patrol the streets of the city to reduce the incidents of civil crime and violence.

6. _____ Augustus developed three military units: the Praetorian Guard, the Urban Cohorts, and the Watchmen, also known as the *Vigiles*.

7. _____ The Praetorian Guard was made up of *libertini* from the legions.

8. _____ Although the Praetorian Guard did not have any specific civic duties, it could be called upon in time of crisis to help maintain order.

9. _____ The leaders of the Praetorian Guard, known as praetors, became more and more powerful.

10. _____ The leader of the Urban Cohorts, the Urban Prefect, was entrusted with the task of keeping the city safe from the threat of fire.

11. _____ The firefighters, known as *vigiles*, were *libertini*, or legally freed slaves, under the leadership of centurions and tribunes from the regular army.

12. _____ All three military units lived together in a camp outside the city walls.

13. _____ *Vigiles* had no bodily protection and carried no weapons on their patrols.

14. _____ Buckets of water were all that was used to stop a fire from spreading.

15. _____ Victims of crimes that we consider criminal offenses today, such as theft and assault, were responsible for bringing the offenders into civil court to sue them for damages.

16. _____ Conspiracy, participation in civil disturbances or riots, and membership in certain political or religious groups were examples of crimes against the state.

17. _____ Any of the prefects or aediles had the right to arrest, detain, and even brutally beat an evildoer.

18. _____ Slaves who had committed serious offenses could be forced to work in ships' galleys or face wild beasts in the arena.

19. _____ The worst punishment for a law-breaker was to be forced to fight as a gladiator in the arena.

20. _____ A slave convicted of a capital crime was typically sentenced to crucifixion.

APPREHENDING CRIMINALS

Who was responsible for arresting someone who . . .

1. destroyed the carriage of a businessman? _____

2. stole jewelry from a woman? _____

3. joined a conspiracy plot? _____

4. poisoned drinking water from an aqueduct? _____

5. was a member of a banned religious cult? _____

6. robbed money from a house? _____

7. damaged the reputation of a public figure? _____

8. threatened the life of the emperor? _____

9. punched a man in a fight? _____

10. dismantled a section of a city bridge? _____

IDENTIFY THE UNIT

Below are facts about the Practorian Guard, the Urban Cohorts, and the *Vigiles*, the three military units that protected Rome against crime, violence, and the threat of fire. Read each entry and then decide which unit it describes.

1. This unit most closely resembled the police force of today. _____

2. The primary function of this unit was to fight fires. _____

3. This unit was entrusted with the responsibility of guarding the life of the Roman emperor. _____

4. These two units probably lived in the same camp just outside the city walls. _____

5. Most of the members of this unit were *libertini*. _____

6. One activity of the leader of this unit was to gather intelligence information to help his men maintain order throughout the city. _____

7. The leaders of this unit attained such power that several times throughout the course of Roman history they were responsible for the assassination of an emperor.

             _____

8. The members of this unit lived in stations located in the 14 regions of the city.

             _____

9. This unit was made up of elite legionary soldiers.

             _____

10. This unit was positioned throughout the city so that its men had ready access to major city streets and city walls.

             _____

QUESTIONS FOR THOUGHT AND RESEARCH

1. It may seem strange that there was no police force in ancient Rome, and even stranger that the wealthy, who had more to lose as a result of criminal behavior, did not want a police force. What factors contributed to this situation?

2. Explain why the organization of the *Vigiles* was effective.

3. Research how early Americans fought fires and compare their techniques to those of the *Vigiles*.

4. Many communities have instituted programs called "neighborhood watch." Research this approach to crime control and compare it to the situation in the very early days of ancient Rome, when the population was still small.

ACTIVITIES

1. Interview or write to a firefighter and ask what effective firefighting methods could be employed using only the equipment of the *Vigiles*: blankets, buckets, pikes, axes, ropes, ladders, water, sand, and vinegar.

2. Interview or write to a member of the police force and ask him or her about the difficulties of apprehending criminals and about informing criminals of their rights.

3. Interview or write to a judge and ask about the civil and criminal court structure.

4. Interview an employee of the Secret Service to ask how elected officials are protected.

5. Interview or write to a member of the Secret Service and ask how they protect elected officials.

CHAPTER 11: FARMING

The city of Rome was a busy metropolis whose inhabitants, rich and poor, enjoyed the advantages and endured the disadvantages of life in a densely populated urban capital. Yet the earliest Romans were farmers, and agriculture remained the basis of Rome's economy. The wealthiest families in Rome had homes both in the city and in the country, and wealth was determined by the amount and quality of farmland a family possessed. Farms, both large and small, covered the countryside. They ranged from tiny plots of land with only a few workers to massive, slave-operated factory farms.

SMALL FARMS AND FARMHOUSES

The smallest farms had as little as four acres of land and could be managed by the farmer and only one or two slaves. To maximize profits, every bit of land on these simple farms was usually cultivated. Because most farmers chose not to waste their precious farmland by building a farmhouse on fertile ground, they built their homes in nearby villages and commuted to work. In fact, archaeologists have unearthed only a few small Roman farmhouses, most of which are in the outlying Roman provinces of Germany and Britain, where there were comparatively fewer villages than in Italy. Since evidence about this type of dwelling is so rare, it is difficult to generalize about the nature of small Roman farmhouses.

VILLAE RUSTICAE

Mid-size farms generally contained a modest residence, either for the owner or for the resident overseer. Known as a *villa rustica*, this type of farm and country residence complex normally consisted of an enclosed farmyard and several buildings, including slave dormitories and prison-like structures for locking up slaves (even the smallest operation of this type required several dozen slaves), animal barns, work areas for processing the produce, and storage space. Several spacious and attractively deco-rated living quarters, clearly intended to serve as a residence for the owner and his family, indicate that *villae rusticae* often served both as an active agricultural enterprise and as a country home for the family. Other *villae rusticae* were built solely for country living. Although there is evidence of extensive gardens, there appears to have been no agricultural activity at all.

LATIFUNDIA

As Rome expanded and acquired new territories and slaves, a few of the more prosperous farmers began to buy up smaller farms and convert them into large, efficient operations worked entirely by slaves and their overseers. These large farms, known as *latifundia*, gradually dominated the farming industry and made the career of farming difficult, if not impossible, for small farmers.

Fig. 44.
This reconstructed villa at Xanten, Germany shows the wide variety of plants grown by the Romans.

WORKING FARMS

Ancient literature, images in ancient art, and the remains of farm tools and buildings unearthed by archaeologists provide clues about Roman farming practices. Romans knew how to adapt their crops to different types of soil and terrain. They maximized fertility by allowing land periodically to lie fallow, by rotating crops, and by combining crops. They understood the principles of water control and made use of drainage and irrigation. They cultivated olive trees, grape vines and vegetable gardens. And they developed an efficient system of harvesting and storing produce, especially grain and beans.

Slaves, under the direction of an overseer, himself often a slave, performed nearly all of the routine tasks. Livestock was an essential part of every farm. Oxen were harnessed to heavy farm equipment and horses and donkeys were used for lighter chores and as beasts of burden. And, of course, other farm animals were kept as food-producing livestock. Because of the abundance of animals on a farm, farmers needed to reserve a large portion of their land for the growing and storing of fodder.

PROCESSING AND STORING

In a world without refrigeration, food that spoiled easily was consumed fresh and could not be transported long distances. Much of the produce, however, could be processed and packaged to extend its shelf life and then transported long distances by land and sea. Grains, nuts and legumes were separated from their non-edible parts, dried, and sealed into earthenware containers.

American Academy in Rome, Photographic Archive

Fig. 45.
Donkeys were important farm animals and were used as beasts of burden or harnessed to light farm equipment and carts.

Fig. 46.
Workers unload heavy *amphorae* as record-keepers tally the shipment.

Presses turned perishable olives into oil, and crushers processed grapes into concentrate used to make wine and vinegar. Similarly, processed milk products, most notably cheese, if properly stored, lasted a long time.

LIVESTOCK

The Romans raised a variety of animals. Besides the expected assortment of farm animals, such as cows, goats, sheep, pigs, and chickens, Romans also farmed fish and mollusks, such as trout and oysters, edible rodents, such as dormice, and often kept bees. Cattle and goats were raised for milk and cheese, horses and pigs for meat, sheep for wool, and poultry for eggs.

American Academy in Rome, Photographic Archive

Fig. 47.
Shepherds took care of flocks of sheep and often worked for the master of a large farm.

Fig. 48.
Bakeries used millstones like these to grind their own grain for bread.

Older, surplus, or unproductive animals were slaughtered for meat. Some meat was salted, smoked or dried for storage or shipment but, as a rule, animals were transported alive as long as possible. Fish were raised in impressive fisheries, primarily in southern Italy and in Spain, but much of that industry was devoted to raising expensive luxury items, such as eels and oysters, or to supply the raw materials for the manufacture of a fermented fish sauce, called *garum* or *liquamen*, that was used throughout the Mediterranean world. This sauce, used much as we use ketchup or mustard, was stored in jars and was easily transported. Large evaporation tanks, used to collect sea salt for preservation and seasoning, have been found on some farms.

American Academy in Rome, Photographic Archive

Fig. 49.
Horses were harnessed to millstones and forced to walk around in circles to rotate the mechanism that ground the grain.

MARKETING

All of these products were passed on to suppliers and to consumers in Rome and in the towns and villages of Italy and in the provinces. Every town required extensive granaries to store the grain that would eventually be ground to flour and baked into bread. Produce was sold in a marketplace or *forum*, sometimes by the farmer, sometimes through a middleman. A small town might have just one market, but larger towns, like Rome, had a vegetable market, a cattle market, and a fish market.

Chapter 11 Exercises: *Farming*

TRUE OR FALSE

Indicate whether each statement is true or false. If it is false, identify the error and correct it.

1. _____ Because the Italian soil was so dry, the earliest Romans imported most of the food they consumed.

2. _____ We know a great deal about life on small farms from the numerous surviving remains of small Roman farmhouses.

3. _____ A working, mid-sized farm complex was called a *villa rustica*.

4. _____ *Villae rusticae* were built solely as working farms.

5. _____ As Rome expanded and conquered more people, slaves flooded the markets and enabled the wealthy to buy up small farms and to create large-scale, slave-operated farms.

6. _____ Large farms were known as *latifundia*.

7. _____ The spread of *latifundia* posed no threat to small farmers, whose high-quality produce commanded higher prices in Roman markets.

8. _____ Romans had no knowledge of crop rotation and consequently were unable to maximize the fertility of the soil.

9. _____ Farming was a full-time job for the farm owner who had to be present at all times to direct the work and to manage the slaves.

10. _____ Horses were used to pull plows and other heavy farm equipment.

11. _____ Although the Romans knew how to preserve meat, they were unable to preserve grains, nuts, and legumes.

12. _____ Romans cultivated and ate rodents.

13. _____ Along with other animals raised on farms, such as chickens, sheep, goats, and pigs, Romans cultivated fish and mollusks.

14. _____ Roman fish sauce, called *garum* or *liquamen*, was a rare and expensive luxury food item because it was so difficult to transport.

15. _____ Produce was sold in a marketplace, called a *forum*.

CROSSWORD PUZZLE

Across

4. The practice of watering crops
6. Mid-sized farms
9. Used to make wine and vinegar
10. An animal used for lighter farm work
11. Another name for the popular fish sauce the Romans called *liquamen*
12. One way to preserve meat (Hint: there are two possible answers.)
13. Large-scale, factory farms

Down

1. Farm animals that provide milk and cheese
2. The basis of Rome's economy
3. Food for animals
5. One way to maximize the fertility of the soil
7. Peas and beans, for example
8. Animals harnessed to heavy farm equipment

SHORT ANSWERS

Answer the following questions in the space provided.

1. Explain why it made better sense for the owners of small farms to live in nearby villages and travel to work.

2. Name some of the different fields of study that have provided us with clues about Roman farming practices and techniques.

3. Name five different types of areas or structures that were typically found on the grounds of a *villa rustica*.

4. Explain how the increased availability of land and slaves contributed to the rise of *latifundia*.

5. Describe some ways that Romans could extend the shelf life of their food and produce.

Word Study

1. *Villa* is the Latin word for a large house. The Latin adjective *rustica* means "of the country." A *villa rustica*, then, was a large country house. Originally it referred to the farmhouse or headquarters of a large working farm. Eventually wealthy Romans began to build country estates, without working farms, for the pleasure of living in the country. And so the term meant a large country farmhouse or just a large country house.

    How many English words can you think of that derive from the Latin words *villa* or *rustica*?

2. A *latifundium* is term that is made up of two Latin root words. *Latus* is a Latin adjective meaning "wide" and *fundus* is a noun that means "base," "bottom" or "foundation." And so a big farm was literally something with a wide or expansive base or ground.

    How many English words can you think of that derive from the Latin words *latus* and *fundus*?

3. Mollusks such as snails, mussels, and especially oysters were delicacies for the Romans. Archaeologists have found the remains on farms of elaborate ponds used to cultivate oysters. Mollusks are invertebrates, or creatures that have no bone structure. The soft bodies of mollusks are protected by their shells. The word "mollusk" comes from the Latin adjective *mollis* that means "soft."

    How many English words can you find that derive from the Latin word *mollis*?

4. Legumes are seeds that grow in pods. Pods are long cases that split along their outside edges when ripe, revealing a row of seeds, such as peas or beans, attached to one edge of the pod. Although the origin of the word legume is not clear, some authorities think it is related to the Latin verb *legere* that means "to gather." Peas and beans can be scooped or gathered easily from their pods.

    Most Latin verbs have four parts. The four parts of *legere* are: *lego, legere, legi, lectum*.

    How many English words can you think of that derive from the Latin verb *legere*?

5. Wine is made from pressed grapes whose juice was concentrated, fermented and aged. Once the process was complete, the concentrate had to be diluted with water before it could be consumed. At Roman dinner parties, the guests rolled dice to determine who would decide how much water should be added to the concentrate to make the wine taste just right. Linguists tell is that in Latin the consonant "v" was pronounced like our "w." (The Latin alphabet did not have the letter "w.") In Latin, the word for wine is *vinum*.

The word "vintage" can be used both as a noun and as an adjective. Can you give the meaning of each use of the word vintage and explain how this word relates to the process of making wine?

FURTHER RESEARCH

1. It is difficult for us to imagine life without refrigeration. Salting, smoking, and drying were three ways that Romans preserved their food. Research the chemical effects of these processes on food.

2. We have many different options open to us for acquiring food produced on farms. Investigate some of the ways that the food we eat reaches our tables. Visit a local farmers' market, a small, independent grocery store, or a large supermarket and interview a person in charge of selling produce (fruit and vegetables), dairy products, or meat. Find out how many steps are involved in bringing the food from the farm to the store.

3. Look through a cookbook and find a recipe that you think could have been prepared in ancient Rome. Make a dish and bring it to class.

CHAPTER 12:
OCCUPATIONS

INTRODUCTION

Ancient Romans, like people of today, engaged in a wide variety of occupations. There were shopkeepers, manual laborers, artisans, soldiers, secretaries, teachers, doctors, lawyers, and politicians, to name a few. The reasons that motivated members of each social class to work hard were varied. Patricians and nobles, usually offspring of the wealthiest families, considered it beneath their dignity to work for money. Although they received no monetary compensation, they worked hard at their professions for the good of the community and for the personal satisfaction that comes from earning the respect and acclaim of their fellow Romans. Business-minded equestrians, as a rule, wanted to earn enough money to compete socially with other members of the upper class. And hardworking ex-slaves, both skilled and unskilled, hoped to improve the quality of their life and to earn acceptance into Roman society.

Fig. 50.
In this relief a vendor sells his wares.

ARISTOCRATS, NOBLES, AND POLITICAL LIFE

By law, the Roman aristocracy and senatorial class were not permitted to engage in any business other than farming. Since the majority of these Romans came from wealthy families, such a restriction did not normally cause financial hardship. Those members of the upper class who did not have income-producing land and were in need of money, however, had several options. Some pursued the study of law. Although Roman lawyers were not permitted to charge fees for their services in court, they often received generous gifts from their satisfied clients. Some joined the army and amassed huge personal fortunes from the spoils of war. Others served as magistrates in the provinces, where fraud and the dishonest collection of tax money were both commonplace and financially lucrative. Still others illegally engaged in income-earning activities (especially shipping and money lending), using their clients and ex-slaves as agents.

Honest and financially secure nobles and aristocrats were seldom idle. They spent most of their time and energy serving the interests of the state as politicians, army officers, and religious magistrates. Although no salary was attached to these high positions and holding them often involved considerable personal expense, nevertheless they were eagerly sought.

During the Republic, when power was in the hands of elected officials, the political arena was marked by fierce competition. The quest of all serious politicians was to be elected to the highest position, that of *consul*. Family connections were an important asset for success. In the last century of the Republic, for example, half the number of consuls came from only ten families. Two consuls were elected each year and they shared their power. Consuls convened the Senate, which served as an advisory body. They led legions into battle during times of war, and they established policy during peacetime. But comparatively few politicians achieved their goal of becoming a *consul*.

Although the preliminary steps to becoming a *consul* were never strictly formalized by law, Romans were expected to pursue a political stepladder or career path of preliminary offices known as the *cursus honorum*, or "course of honors." This series of offices usually included the positions of *quaestor, aedile*, and *praetor*, but it was certainly politically advantageous for an aspiring *consul*, depending on his class, also to have served as military tribune or plebeian tribune.

Each office trained the politician for a different aspect of effective urban or military administration. A politician could perform the duties of each preliminary office in the city of Rome itself, in the towns and municipalities of Italy, or in the outlying provinces. Every candidate for public office was expected to finance his own campaign.

Once elected, a *quaestor* was primarily a minister of finance who was responsible for collecting taxes, both in the form of money and, in some cases, grain and for depositing the resources he collected in the treasury and storage houses of Rome. Although the office of *aedile* was not officially a step in the *cursus honorum*, most consuls held this office. An *aedile* took care of the city. He made sure that public works, such as roads, bridges, and aqueducts were properly maintained. He supervised the distribution of the daily allotment of grain to the poor. He also managed the celebration of religious rites and provided, at his own expense, public entertainment in the form of banquets, games, and spectacles. The office of *aedile* offered a would-be *consul* ample opportunity to win the favor of the masses by providing them with lavish forms of amusement. A *praetor* was second in command to the consuls and, as such, performed almost all the duties of consuls in their absence. Special urban praetors were placed in charge of legal matters and, as judges, they heard and passed judgment on legal cases brought before them. And so, having held the offices of *quaestor, aedile*, and *praetor*, an ambitious politician could present himself as a candidate for the consulship with demonstrated expertise in financial matters, the maintenance of public works, the planning of public events, and in administering the law.

Prior to these major offices, candidates for the consulship often served as military tribune or plebeian tribune. After five years of military service, a soldier could be elected or appointed military tribune within his legion. He was responsible for the behavior and welfare of his fellow soldiers and he was generally in charge of the day-to-day aspects of camp life. The plebeian tribune, on the other hand, was an urban political officer elected by an assembly of plebeians. Their major responsibility was to safeguard the rights of the plebeian class. They held the power of veto and could use it to block any action proposed by a magistrate.

After a Roman held the office of *praetor* or *consul*, he became eligible to serve as *propraetor* or *proconsul* of a province. In this capacity he assumed the governorship of a province assigned to him by the Senate. He could also serve as *censor* within the city. The most important responsibilities of a *censor* were to keep the census rolls up to date and to enforce the laws and standards of proper behavior.

Priests in ancient Rome, except for the priestesses of the goddess Vesta, were often, but not exclusively, men from the upper class. They were members of religious colleges or brotherhoods. Serving as a priest was a civic as well as a religious responsibility. Priests organized and performed the numerous religious rites and festivals that filled the ancient Roman calendar, although the funding for these events came from the state. The Senate often consulted the most important religious colleges when making decisions that affected religious matters. The highest religious office was that of *Pontifex Maximus,* or Chief Priest.

EQUESTRIANS AND POLITICAL LIFE

The members of the equestrian class were often just as wealthy as the aristocracy. If an equestrian chose to pursue a political career and was elected to high public office, he was called a *novus homo,* or a "self-made man," because he had gone beyond the expectations of his class. In this case, a *novus homo* was required to adhere to the work restrictions that applied to his aristocratic colleagues.

Equestrians who did not pursue the political life could engage in any occupation they wished. And many financially successful equestrians amassed huge fortunes. Some came from old families, but others were from families recently enrolled as citizens. To become a member of the equestrian class, one needed to meet certain minimum wealth requirements. Some equestrians acquired their wealth through banking and money-lending, collecting taxes in the provinces for a percentage of the yield, or through large-scale shipping and trading enterprises. Since relatively few equestrians entered public life, we know less about this group of Romans than about their aristocratic counterparts.

During the empire, a separate *cursus honorum* for the equestrians was established to encourage their participation in public service. The offices opened to them included tribune, *curator* (a position similar to that of *aedile*), and *procurator* (a governor, similar to the position of *proconsul*). But the steps for advancement to the highest equestrian office, that of Prefect of the Praetorian Guard, were less clearly defined than those for advancement to the office of *consul*. The prefect of the Praetorian Guard was in charge of the elite forces that protected the general. During the Empire, the praetorian guards protected the emperor.

TRADESPEOPLE AND PROFESSIONALS

Many professional careers, such as undertakers, auctioneers, architects, medical doctors, and teachers were not highly regarded by the Romans. These occupations, though important, did not provide a good income. In general, foreigners and ex-slaves practiced these professions.

Romans frequently formed associations or burial clubs, similar to medieval guilds, called *collegia*. Members were people who worked in the same trade. Surviving inscriptions record the activities of *collegia* of tanners, cobblers, carpenters, smiths, potters, dyers, midwives, and even flute players. Since these people were generally not wealthy, their membership dues in the *collegia* were used to insure the eventual cost of their own funeral banquet and burial. *Collegia* were also a source of social activities that offered a sense of camaraderie for their members. Some tradespeople and professionals earned enough money in their lifetimes to build impressive tombs, featuring carved scenes pertaining to their occupations. In fact, these burial monuments can be an important source of information about the occupations of the Romans they commemorate.

Fig. 51.
A butcher commemorated his trade and his tools on his tomb.

Fig. 52.
This tavern at Ostia was the equivalent of today's "fast food" restaurants.

Tradespeople provided the basic commodities and services necessary for everyday life in ancient Rome. There were taverns, bakeries, butcher shops, dry cleaners, and moneylenders, to name a few. Merchants also offered luxury goods, such as jewelry, books, and works of art. The names of certain streets in Rome and references to activities that took place on others indicate that people of the same profession tended to cluster together. For example, we know that one area of Rome contained a road called the Street of the Scythe Makers, and that booksellers could be found on a street called the *Argiletum,* near the Roman Forum. Downtown Rome abounded in narrow streets lined with small shop fronts.

American Academy in Rome, Photographic Archive

Fig. 53.
A market scene in which merchants sell poultry, bread, and pet monkeys. The frieze may be in honor of the second man from the left who appears to be an official in charge of public markets.

THE URBAN POOR

We can only imagine what life was like for the masses of poor people. The abundance of slaves made employment opportunities scarce for unskilled workers. Low wages forced many to live in shabby dwellings or to become homeless. But the daily distribution of free grain to the poor kept these citizens from starving. And those fortunate to have a patron often received additional gifts of food and the possibility of employment. Certainly the city of Rome had its share of beggars and thieves. Many Roman citizens chose to join the army.

Fig. 54.
Two legionaries prepare to do battle.

THE ROMAN ARMY

Originally, Roman soldiers were small farmers drafted to serve. But in the Late Republic Rome began to support a professional army. The army was comprised of a standing force of legions made up of men who enlisted for a period of 16 to 25 years and who served wherever they were needed. During the Empire, Roman soldiers were stationed at the borders of Roman provinces and territories. They either extended the boundaries or strengthened them against the attacks of hostile neighbors. During this period, the Roman army had a strong presence in places such as Egypt, Britain, and along the Rhine, Danube and Euphrates rivers.

Life in the army could be dangerous, but to a poor urban dweller it offered food, shelter and a reliable source of income. Although soldiers were not legally permitted to marry, many did raise families on the frontier. It was not uncommon for a soldier eventually to retire with a savings, a bonus, and a small grant of land. All that was required to become a Roman soldier after the Late Republic was Roman citizenship and good health. Non-citizens were permitted to enlist in the auxiliary cohorts or in the navy.

Since the Roman style of combat was physically demanding and required proficiency in handling a variety of weapons and tools, a legionary soldier underwent a long and grueling regimen of training and discipline. On campaign, a soldier was expected to march long distances carrying heavy loads. Each night he helped to build a temporary camp, fortified by ditches and earthen walls with wooden palisades. In the morning, he and his fellow soldiers demolished the camp and marched to the next campsite or went straight into battle.

An army was divided into legions, normally consisting of between 4,200 and 6,000 men. A legion was subdivided into ten cohorts. A cohort, in turn, was subdivided into several centuries of about 80 men each. The officers in charge of each century were called *centuriones*. These were common soldiers who had risen from the ranks. It was the responsibility of a *centurio* or centurion to lead his century or cohort into battle.

Typically, a Roman army lined up facing the enemy. When the general gave the order to advance, soldiers marched silently in formation until they came within 100 feet of the enemy. Then they launched volleys of heavy javelins into the enemy lines, usually with devastating effect. As they came closer to the enemy, they drew their short swords, beat them against their large curved shields, and shouted a war cry, such as *Vae victis*! (Woe to the conquered!). Their tight, synchronized formations, their short thrusting swords, and maneuverability usually made short work of the enemy. A smart commander always made sure that his soldiers shared in the spoils of war.

Some soldiers never participated in active combat. Instead, they built and protected Roman forts and garrisons on the frontier. They also helped to build new permanent camps, roads, and aqueducts. They served as peacekeepers, administrators, and tax collectors. When they retired, they often settled nearby and helped to further civilize and Romanize the area. Many modern cities and towns of Britain and Germany were originally Roman camps.

Chapter 12 Exercises: *Occupations*

WHO AM I?

From the box below, select the title that best describes each character.

quaestor	*aedile*	*praetor*
consul	*censor*	military tribune
plebeian tribune	*Pontifex Maximus*	*novus homo*
proconsul	prefect of the Praetorian Guard	

1. I hold the highest religious office. My title means that I am a "bridge-builder" between the world of mortals and the world of gods. _____

2. I hold the highest office entrusted to a member of the equestrian class. I command the force of men whose duty is to protect the life of our emperor. _____

3. I have served in the Roman army for five years. During that time, I earned the respect of my fellow soldiers, who selected me to be the person in charge of making our life in camp run smoothly. I look out for the well-being of my men, and I expect them to behave as good Roman soldiers should. _____

4. My patrician heart beats with pride as I stroll around our beautiful city and see the masterpieces of Roman engineering in good working order. It is my responsibility to insure the efficient operation of our bridges, roads, and aqueducts. I also make sure the poor are given bread to eat, and I plan and carry out large-scale public entertainment to amuse the masses and to increase my own popularity. _____

5. I have made my family proud of me. Although I am an equestrian, I have earned the respect of the people who have elected me consul. My cousin will take over my lucrative import-export business since, by law, I am no longer permitted to engage in business pursuits. I am honored to serve my people and my country. _____

6. Honestly! People these days need constant reminders about proper appearance and behavior. When I was consul, a shocking number of senators attended senate meetings with togas sloppily draped and wearing far too much jewelry. I worry about the examples adults today are setting for our children. _____

7. My family always taught me to speak up and to defend those people with less power. Needless to say, I am pleased that the members of the lower class have elected me to be the guardian of their rights. In my new position, I will not hesitate to use my veto power to block any measure that threatens the rights of the lower class. _____

8. Well, it wasn't easy, but after completing all the offices of the *cursus honorum*, I have reached the top. Fortunately, my colleague in office and I agree about how this land should be governed. We plan to convene the Senate early next week to seek their advice about improving the tax laws.

    _____

9. Work, work, work! That's all I do. Not only do I have a backlog of legal cases to judge but, because the consuls have been away so much, I have had all of their work to do. Just yesterday I convened the Senate because the issues were too pressing to wait for the consuls' return. _____

10. I know it is difficult for people to pay their taxes, but the system is fair. After all, how else can Rome provide public services for its people? Their taxes are used to build and maintain roads, aqueducts, and bridges, to feed the hungry poor, and to be prepared financially for the threat of war. It is my job to make sure the treasury of Rome is filled. _____

11. Who would have thought that after my stellar year as consul, the Senate would assign me to be governor of this little province. But I must not complain. I will serve my country with honor and dignity. _____

Matching Columns

Match the letter of the entry in the second column with the correct word(s) in the first column.

1. _____ aristocrats and senators   a) an equestrian consul

2. _____ equestrian   b) prerequisites for a consul

3. _____ non-citizen soldiers   c) forbidden to earn income except from farming

4. _____ *cursus honorum*   d) divisions of a legion

5. _____ *Vae victis*   e) prerequisites for a legionary soldier

6. _____ *novus homo*   f) prefect of the Praetorian Guard

7. _____ citizenship and good health   g) advisory body

8. _____ senate   h) auxiliary troops and navy

9. _____ *collegia*   i) battle cry

10. _____ cohorts and centuries   j) burial clubs

Short Answers

Answer the following questions in the space provided.

1. Give some reasons that motivated members of each social class (aristocrats, equestrians, and plebeians) to work hard at their jobs.

2. What options for earning income were open to those holders of high public office who did not own income-producing land?

3. Briefly discuss the *cursus honorum*. What was it? Why was it a good idea?

4. Who served as priests and what did they do?

5. How did one become a member of the equestrian class?

6. Name some types of activities that equestrians engaged in to earn income.

7. Explain the nature and function of Roman *collegia*.

8. What measures and practices helped the poorest citizens of Rome to survive?

9. For how long was a Roman soldier's tour of duty?

10. What were daily chores of a soldier on campaign?

11. Describe how a clash between the Roman army and the enemy generally began.

FOR DISCUSSION

1. Discuss the pros and cons of the *cursus honorum*. If you could create a *cursus honorum* in your school, what offices and requirements would it include? Do you think the American system of government should have a *cursus honorum*? Why? What would it include?

2. Discuss the pros and cons of salaries for public officials.

3. Discuss the pros and cons of a military career.

4. In ancient Rome, people of the same profession tended to cluster together. Find examples of areas in cities today where people of the same profession practice their trade.

5. Identify some modern versions of Roman *collegia*.

CHAPTER 13: TRAVEL AND TRADE

INTRODUCTION

Romans excelled in the building of roads. They also constructed harbors and developed sea routes. Although travel in and around the ancient Mediterranean was never quick and easy, and was frequently dangerous, still the Romans were justifiably proud of their accomplishments. People, products, and information moved back and forth freely across a vast and sophisticated network of land and sea routes and eventually extended to the outermost reaches of the Roman Empire.

Fig. 55.
Two trading ships flank a lighthouse on this pavement in front of the offices of a shipping company in the port city of Ostia.

MAPS

The Romans had a fairly good idea of what their world looked like. The few surviving stone representations of the city of Rome and of the known world show that the Romans were aware of geography. There must have been many other examples on less durable media. Their maps surely did not resemble ours, but Romans certainly had a sense of location and distance.

Fig. 56.
This picture shows a stretch of the ancient *Via Appia*, parts of which are still in use today.

ROADS

The oldest Roman road was the *Via Appia*, built under the supervision of Appius Claudius in 312 BCE. Called the *Regina Viarum*, or "the Queen of Roads," the *Via Appia* stretched from Rome south to Capua. Later the *Via Appia* was extended to Brundisium, affording easy access to the seaport there and facilitating travel to and from Greece. Some sections of the *Via Appia* are still in use today.

By the end of the third century CE the Romans had at their disposal a network of roads measuring 53,000 miles (85,000 km). Most of these roads were originally built by and for the Roman army, since soldiers could march farther and faster on a hard, flat, and well-drained surface.

The construction team first dug two parallel furrows that served as drainage ditches on either side of the roadway. The area between was excavated to firm soil or bedrock to a depth of 4.6 feet (1.4 meters). Next a loosely packed layer of stones was added to allow for drainage from the upper layers. Then dirt and rock, excavated when the furrows were dug, were spread to form the next layer. This layer was packed hard and further strengthened by ramming devices. Finally, the top layer, consisting of gravel or, if available, large, cut stones was added. The center of the road was slightly curved to permit easy drainage of water.

Fig. 57.
The raised sidewalks show that city streets helped to drain water toward the sewer system.

Fig. 58.
Roman roads had deep foundations and were paved with large durable stones to handle centuries of wheeled traffic.

In areas inhabited by potentially hostile people, trees along the edges of the road were cleared to prevent ambushes. Roads generally followed the natural curve of the terrain, but wherever possible they were laid as straight as possible. This allowed for greater speed of construction and ease of travel. At every 1,000 paces a *miliarium* or milestone was erected. On it were inscribed the distances to the nearest towns and sometimes the distance from Rome, measured from the golden milestone in the Roman Forum.

BRIDGES

In the outer reaches of the provinces, the Roman army on the march cut tunnels through hills and mountains and built bridges over rivers. Since speed was usually of primary importance, these bridges were made of wood. Oftentimes they were later replaced by stone versions. In the city of Rome, the *Pons Fabricius*, the stone bridge built in 62 BCE that links the left bank of the Tiber to Tiber Island, still stands.

Fig. 59.
This view of Tiber Island shows, in the distance, the *Pons Fabricius*, built in 62 BCE.

Roman bridges usually rise steeply in the middle since the central arch, which bore the weight of the bridge from below, was semicircular. Foundations for bridges were sunk into the riverbed. Wooden boxes called coffers were built where the foundations were to be placed. Water was pumped out of the coffers so that foundation stones could be sunk into the riverbed and piers could be built while the area inside the coffer was relatively dry. Then the water was let back in.

Stone barriers were usually built to reduce the force of the flow of water around the foundations and to lessen the possibility of damage from floating objects. The cement used in the construction of Roman bridges was waterproof. Many ancient Roman stone and brick bridges have survived.

TRAVEL BY LAND

Roads were initially constructed to facilitate the movement of the Roman army. Foot soldiers carried most of their own equipment and food on their backs. Wheeled vehicles followed the marching army and transported additional supplies and heavy equipment. Once the roads were built, non-military personnel, like travelers and messengers, also used them. Private couriers were hired to carry letters on foot or by horse. And the state-operated *cursus publicus* was the Roman equivalent of the Pony Express or a stagecoach company.

To accommodate the increasing number of travelers, stations were set up every twenty or thirty miles where animals were exchanged and couriers could rest. Usually there was an inn nearby. Ancient Roman travelers walked on the roads, or rode a horse or even a mule. Sometimes they were transported in a *lectica* carried by slaves, or they rode in a private or hired carriage. Wheeled vehicles did not have shock absorbers or springs, and long distance travel was undoubtedly uncomfortable.

Loads were transported in several ways. Slaves carried packs, pulled wagons, or supported litters laden with goods. Horses and mules were used as transport animals. Oxen were yoked to carts or wagons. Since the horse collar and the horseshoe had not been invented, mules and horses did not pull heavy wagons, nor could they travel long distances over paved surfaces. Land routes were not an economical means for transporting large or heavy loads.

TRAVEL BY SEA

The Mediterranean Sea, called *Mare Nostrum* or "Our Sea" by the Romans, was a superhighway connecting all the lands that bordered it and even cities located near navigable rivers that emptied into it. Then as now, the Mediterranean was relatively tranquil compared to the Atlantic Ocean or the Black Sea, although contrary winds and sudden squalls could make sailing dangerous. A greater danger was piracy. Pirates roamed the seas and preyed on merchant vessels until the threat was all but eliminated during the Late Republic. But perhaps the greatest obstacle of all to a safe voyage was the design of the ships themselves. They were small and not easily maneuverable.

Although warships were sleek, fast, and propelled by large numbers of oarsmen, merchant vessels, designed to carry cargo, were small and round-bottomed and employed

Fig. 60.
Heavily loaded merchant ships which navigated the large rivers of Europe sometimes required oars.

square sails for propulsion. Because these ships had neither keels nor multiple sails, sea captains were unable to steer into the wind or change course easily. The speed and destination of an ancient ship were limited by design and weather conditions. Nevertheless, the sea remained the most economical and reliable means of transporting heavy merchandise.

Fig. 61.
These *amphorae*, retrieved from an ancient shipwreck and covered with barnacles, once stored wine and olive oil.

Cargo ships were well suited for transporting both heavy, bulky materials like metal, stone, and lumber and also smaller, lighter freight, such as grain, oil, and wine. Grain was packed in sacks or barrels, liquids in large terracotta vessels called *amphorae*. These jars could be stowed in the hold of a small ship very efficiently, as has been demonstrated by the discovery of several ancient shipwrecks. Scientific analysis of the contents of ancient cargoes reveals that much of the wine destined for Rome came from France, olive oil from Spain, and grain from Egypt and the Black Sea. Ships also brought other necessities and luxuries to Rome, such as slaves, cloth, and spices.

American Academy in Rome, Photographic Archive

Fig. 62.
This relief shows a cargo ship landing and then the wine it carried served in a tavern.

TRANSPORTING GRAIN

Importing enough grain to feed the huge population of the city of Rome was always a challenge. During the Empire, a public official, known as the Prefect of the Grain Supply, was placed in charge of this important task. Each day of the sailing season an average of 17 ships from the grain-producing provinces of Sicily, North Africa, Egypt and the regions around the Black Sea arrived at Ostia, Rome's seaport. The grain they carried had to be unloaded and transported up the Tiber to Rome. The prefect organized the entire operation. Three thousand laborers unloaded the ships, transferred *amphorae* containing the grain to smaller riverboats, and towed them with teams of oxen up the Tiber to Rome. The cargo was then unloaded into well-ventilated warehouses designed to store huge quantities of grain. From there the grain was sent to neighborhood flourmills and bakeries. The prefect also made sure that loaves of bread were distributed every day, free of charge, to the poor people of the city.

Time and Speed

Travel was possible to any part of the Roman world for those who had the means and the stamina to undertake it. Traveling long distances by land, as we have mentioned, required provisions for replacement animals and rest time. Most travelers by sea paid for transportation on a slow-moving merchant ship. Travel time to destinations beyond the Italian peninsula was calculated in months rather than days and varied according to the season, luck, and the physical health of the traveler. Only the wealthiest Romans traveled for pleasure since, for the average Roman, few journeys were pleasurable experiences.

Chapter 13 Exercises: *Travel and Trade*
FILL IN THE BLANKS
Use the following word bank to fill in the blanks.

Mare Nostrum	messengers	*Via Appia*	travelers
the Roman army	mule	horse collar	keels
travel time	ambushes	milestone	*cursus publicus*
oxen	dam	horse	horseshoe
wood	stone	multiple sails	*amphorae*
waterproof	Brundisium	Rome	Black Sea
Prefect of the Grain Supply	Sicily	North Africa	Egypt
Ostia	Tiber	towed	flourmills

1. The oldest Roman road, known as the Queen of Roads, was the _____. It was extended to provide a southern route from Rome all the way to the seaport of _____, from where a traveler could sail the short distance to Greece.

2. By the end of the third century CE the Romans had built a vast network of roads. Most of these roads were originally built to facilitate the movement of _____. To discourage _____ along roads through dangerous territory, the borders of these roads were usually cleared of trees.

3. Once the roads were built, they were also used by non-military personnel, such as _____ and _____. Private couriers were hired to carry letters on foot or by horse. And the state-operated _____ was the Roman equivalent of a Pony Express or a stagecoach company.

4. At every thousand or so paces a _____, indicating the distance from _____, was set up at the side of the road. Travelers used these as markers to find their way and to calculate _____. Ancient Roman travelers walked on the roads, or rode a _____ or even a _____ but, since the _____ and the _____ had not been invented, these animals could neither pull heavy wagons, nor could they travel long distances over paved surfaces. _____, however, could be yoked to carts and wagons.

5. The earliest Roman bridges were made of _____ and later rebuilt in _____. Foundations for bridges were sunk into the riverbed after it had been exposed by the construction of a _____. The cement used in the construction of Roman bridges was _____.

6. The Mediterranean Sea was called _____ or "Our Sea" by the Romans, who controlled the land and ports that fringed it. But sea travel was not always safe. Since merchant vessels had neither _____ nor _____, sea captains were unable to steer into the wind or change course easily. Cargo ships, however, were well suited for transporting both heavy and light freight. Grain was packed in sacks or barrels, liquids in large terracotta vessels called _____.

7. During the Empire, a public official, known as the _____, was placed in charge of insuring that the city of Rome had enough grain to feed its huge population. Each day of the sailing season an average of 17 ships from the grain-producing provinces of _____, _____, _____ and the regions around the _____ arrived at _____, Rome's seaport. The grain they carried had to be unloaded and transported up the _____ River to Rome. Laborers unloaded the grain onto smaller river boats, and _____ them with teams of oxen to Rome. The cargo was then unloaded into warehouses, from where it was sent to _____ and bakeries for processing. Loaves of bread were distributed every day, free of charge, to the poor people of the city.

FURTHER RESEARCH

1. Investigate the steps involved in building a Roman road and draw a cross-section, labeling each layer.

2. Investigate the steps involved in building a Roman bridge and draw a cross-section and a full view of a typical bridge.

3. Investigate tools and equipment needed for building roads, bridges, and ships. Compare Roman tools and equipment with their counterparts today.

GROUP ACTIVITIES

1. Test your knowledge of geography. Try to draw a map of your town, state, or region without looking at an atlas.

2. Find out the names and destinations of the major Roman roads. Create a map of the Roman Empire that shows the path of each major road. Each group may select one road to research. Include in a group report the answers to the following questions:

    When and by whom was the road built?

    Through what lands and regions did the road pass?

    What, if anything, remains of the road today?

CHAPTER 14: MEASURING TIME AND SPACE

INTRODUCTION

Modern Americans and ancient Romans differed tremendously in their attitudes toward time. The ability to determine a precise moment or measurement of time is important to most Americans. When will the train leave or the bus arrive? How long will the movie or the meeting last? The Romans, on the other hand, were more concerned about marking the occurrence and reoccurrence of broader cycles of time, such as day and night, holidays and ordinary days, business and leisure, planting and harvesting, summer and winter, war and peace.

HOURS

Although the English word "hour" is derived from the Latin word *hora*, the meanings of the two words are quite different. An hour for a Roman was one-twelfth of the available sunlight on any given day, not a block of time consisting of 60 minutes, as it is for us. An hour for a Roman, therefore, was not a fixed but a variable measurement of time. On the day of the summer solstice (the longest day of the year), for example, a Roman hour lasted about 75 minutes (90 minutes at Hadrian's Wall in northern Britain!). By contrast, on the day of the winter solstice (the shortest day of the year), a Roman hour lasted only about 45 minutes (30 minutes at Hadrian's Wall). On the vernal and autumnal equinox, when day and night are equal, a Roman hour, like ours, lasted 60 minutes.

The Roman day began at sunrise (at approximately 6:00 on the day of the equinox). The first hour, then, lasted from 6:00 to 7:00 a.m. because this was the end of the first hour of sunlight. The second hour lasted from 7:00 to 8:00 a.m. and so on. Noon was the end of the sixth hour of the day. At the end of the last hour of daylight, 5:00 to 6:00 p.m., the night watches began.

Fig. 63.
This sundial could accurately measure the hours, but not minutes. The letters indicating the hours are in Greek because it was found in the eastern part of the empire.

Sundials could be relied on for reckoning time only on sunny days. But a sundial showed only approximate times and did not indicate minutes. Of the 256 surviving examples of ancient sundials that mark the seasons and the 12 daylight hours, only one indicates the passage of time in half-hour increments, and none shows a division of time smaller than that.

Romans divided the night into fourths, not twelfths. Each segment represented the amount of time that a sentinel or night watchman was on guard. The first watch lasted from nightfall until halfway to midnight (approximately 9:00 p.m. at the equinox); the second watch began when the first watch ended and lasted until midnight; the third watch lasted from midnight until halfway to dawn (approximately 3:00 a.m. at the equinox); and the fourth watch began when the third watch ended and lasted until dawn.

Romans sometimes made use of a Greek invention, the *clepsydra*, for measuring short periods of time. This was a vessel filled with liquid that dripped out of its container at a fixed rate. Working on the same principle as a sand-filled hour glass, *clepsydrae* measured only about ten to thirty minutes of time and were commonly used to keep track of the length of speeches.

DAYS AND WEEKS

Although the Romans named their months, they did not number the days within each month sequentially, as we do (e.g. April 22 or October 11). Instead, there were three specially indicated days in each month: *Kalendae* (the "Kalends," abbreviated *Kal.*), *Nonae* (the "Nones," abbreviated *Non.*), and *Idus* (the "Ides," abbreviated *Id.*). The Kalends fell on the first day of every month. The Nones were always nine days before the Ides, but the Ides were not always on the same day of each month. The Ides of March, May, July, and October were on the 15th, but in all the other months the Ides fell on the 13th. Romans counted inclusively. That means that they counted the beginning and the end in a series. Since that is true, the Nones of March, May, July, and October fell on the 7th, or nine days (counting inclusively) before the Ides (the 15th day) of those months. In the remaining months of the Roman calendar, the Ides fell on the 13th, and so the Nones of those months fell on the 5th day.

October 15, in the Roman method of recording a date, was written *Id. Oct.*, December 5 was written *Non. Dec.*, and September 1 was written *Kal. Sept.* But what about the days that were not one of the "special" days?

We have already seen that Romans counted backwards from the Ides to arrive at the Nones. In fact, they reckoned all the dates that didn't fall on one of the three special days by counting backwards. If, for example, we want to write February 8th the Roman way, we count backwards from the closest special day beyond the 8th, in this case, the Ides of February (February 13th). If we also remember to count inclusively, we see that February 8th is six days before the Ides of February. A Roman would have used the abbreviation *a.d.* (*ante diem*, or "before the day") to express how many days before a special day a particular date was. And so, a Roman would have written February 8th as *a.d. VI Id. Feb.* or "six days before the Ides of February."

If a date fell on the immediate day before a special day, there was a specific Latin word to indicate this: *pridie* ("the day before," abbreviated *pr.*) February 4, the day before the Nones of February, then, was written *pr. Non. Feb.* (The abbreviation of the names of the months in the Roman calendar are listed below.)

Romans did not count weeks, as we do. The *nundinae* were market days which occurred eight days apart, but they did not consider the days from market day to market day as a block to measure the passage of time. Each day, however, was sacred to a specific god. Beginning with Saturday, the days were sacred to Saturn, the Sun, the Moon, Mars, Mercury, Jupiter, and Venus (*dies Saturni, Solis, Lunae, Martis, Mercurii, Iovis* and *Veneris*).

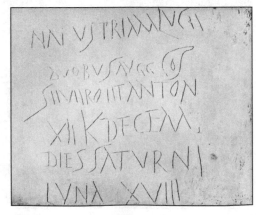

Fig. 64.
The fourth and fifth lines of this inscription read, "XII K DECEM, DIES SATURNI," or 12 days before the Kalends of December, Saturn's day (Saturday, November 20).

MONTHS AND YEARS

In the earliest Roman calendars, months were based on the phases of the moon. Each month lasted approximately 29.5 days, or a complete lunar cycle. The Kalends fell on the day of the new moon and the Ides fell on the day of the full moon. There were only ten lunar months, and the year began in the spring on March 15th. Extra days, and sometimes even months, had to be periodically inserted into the lunar year in order to keep the calendar in harmony with the changing seasons of the longer solar year.

The Ides of March was celebrated as New Year's Day until 152 BCE, when two additional lunar months, January and February, were inserted before the month of March. The first day of the year was shifted back to the Kalends of January. But the names of the pre-existing months remained unchanged. Today, the months of September, October, November, and December remind us that these months were once the seventh, eighth, ninth, and tenth months of the Roman lunar calendar that began in March.

Julius Caesar reformed the calendar in 45 BCE and changed it to a solar calendar. In so doing, he kept twelve months, but increased the number of days in each month to 30 or 31, except February, which continued to have only 28 days. He also added an extra day every four years (our leap year), and renamed the seventh month (*Quinctilis*) Julius after himself.

During Augustus' rule, the month previously known as *Sextilis* was renamed August in his honor. By the beginning of the Empire, then, the Roman year consisted of 12 months named: *Januarius, Februarius, Martius, Aprilis, Maius, Junius, Julius, Augustus, September, October, November,* and *December.* They were usually abbreviated as follows: *Jan., Feb., Mart., Apr., Mai., Jun., Jul., Aug., Sept., Oct., Nov.,* and *Dec.*

Years were often indicated by naming the two consuls who served during that year. So, for example, something that happened in the year 59 BCE (according to our method of calculating years) occurred in the consulships of Caesar and Bibulus. Another method of locating a year in time was to number it from the year of the legendary founding of Rome (or 753 BCE). This was used primarily by historical writers, notably Livy. Thus, for a Roman, an event that occurred in 509 BCE happened in 245 AUC (an abbreviation for *ab urbe condita*, or "from the founding of the city").

In the sixth century, the monk Dionysius Exiguus formulated the familiar and widely-used BC/AD system, using the birth of Jesus as the dividing year. Recently, in an effort to acknowledge non-Christian cultures, the term BC (before Christ) is often replaced with BCE (Before the Common Era) and, instead of the term AD (a Latin abbreviation for *Anno Domini* or "in the year of Our Lord"), the term CE (in the Common Era) is frequently used.

MEASURES OF DISTANCE

Roman milestones were simple stone roadside markers that numbered the miles from one settlement to the next. Fortunately, archaeologists have discovered many Roman milestones in their original locations. By measuring the space between them, we know that a Roman mile measured 1.48 km or .93 miles. The Latin term for a mile is *mille passus,* or "a thousand paces." Simple math, then, tells us that a Roman pace measured 1.48 meters or about 4 feet, 10 inches. Since there are five *pedes* or feet in a pace, a Roman foot was 29.59 cm or 11.6 inches.

In measuring distances with milestones, as in measuring time, Romans were not concerned with absolute accuracy. Rather, milestones helped a traveler to locate a particular place (at the 42nd milestone, for example) and were used to determine the average daily mileage of a traveler, a good way to predict the day of arrival at one's destination.

Similarly, builders and contractors, before beginning a construction project, settled on the measurement of the foot they would use. It didn't matter if it was exactly 29.59 cm, so long as everyone on the job was using the same measurement.

Measures of Weight and Volume

In Rome, certain elected officials were entrusted with the task of ensuring that the merchants in the markets used weights and measures that conformed to official standards. A Roman pound (*libra*) was about 12 ounces. There were other standards used to measure the volumes of solids and liquids.

Chapter 14 Exercises: *Measuring Time and Space*

CONVERSION EXERCISE

Convert the time of day or night in ancient Rome to our equivalent. (Assume that it is the day of the vernal or the autumnal equinox.)

1. The third hour _____

2. The fifth hour _____

3. The second hour _____

4. The eleventh hour _____

5. The ninth hour _____

6. The sixth hour _____

7. The third watch _____

8. The second watch _____

9. The fourth watch _____

10. The first watch _____

Since numbers are the basis of measurement, it is important to learn Roman numerals thoroughly. Romans expressed numbers with alphabetical symbols, known as Roman numerals:

I	=	1
V	=	5
X	=	10
L	=	50
C	=	100
D	=	500
M	=	1,000

Romans did not use fractions, nor did they have a symbol for zero.

The same numerical symbol could be written in succession up to three times. (Sometimes they were written four times, as is often the case with ones on clocks and sundials.) The value of each repeated symbol was added.

A Roman numeral placed to the right of a numeral with a higher value was added to the sum. A single numeral placed to the left of a numeral of greater value was subtracted. (It is important to note, however, that a subtracted numeral must be the same decimal place or one lower decimal place than the numeral from which it is to be subtracted. Thus, the number 99 is written XCIX, or 100 minus ten plus ten minus one. It is not possible to subtract one from one hundred to arrive at 99, since the numeral one is more than one decimal place value less than 100.)

When writing numbers using Roman numerals, it is helpful to build the number from the largest decimal place to the smallest. Thus 1894 is

1,000 (M) + 800 (DCCC) + 90 (XC) + 4 (IV) = MDCCCXCIV

MATCHING COLUMNS

Match each of the following Roman numerals in the first column with its equivalent in the second column

1. _____ XXIII   a) 447
2. _____ IV   b) 1938
3. _____ XLV   c) 56
4. _____ XCII   d) 2001
5. _____ DCCCIX   e) 4
6. _____ LVI   f) 809
7. _____ CDXLVII   g) 1696
8. _____ MCMXXXVIII   h) 23
9. _____ MMI   i) 45
10. _____ MDCXCVI   j) 92

CONVERSION EXERCISE

Convert the following numbers.

1. LXXXIV   _____   1338   _____
2. MCMXXI   _____   48   _____
3. MDCCXCVII   _____   363   _____
4. MDV   _____   2809   _____
5. MCDLXI   _____   753   _____

6. MCMXCIX _____   1776   _____

7. CDIX   _____   2005   _____

8. XVII   _____   97   _____

9. DCCCVI   _____   1066   _____

10. DX   _____   62   _____

Matching Columns

Match each of the following Roman dates in the second column with its equivalent in the first column.

1. _____ April 3   a) a.d. VIII Kal. Mart.

2. _____ July 27   b) a.d. III Kal. Feb.

3. _____ March 14   c) a.d. VI Kal. Aug.

4. _____ February 22   d) Non. Mai.

5. _____ September 5   e) a.d. III Non. Apr.

6. _____ November 12   f) Non. Sept.

7. _____ January 30   g) pr. Kal. Jan.

8. _____ December 31   h) pr. Id. Mart.

9. _____ May 7   i) a.d. XVIII Kal. Jul.

10. _____ August 10   j) pr. Id. Nov.

11. _____ June 14   k) a.d. XV Kal. Nov.

12. _____ October 18   l) a.d. IV Id. Aug.

Conversion Exercise

Convert the following dates.

1. January 4   _____   a.d. XI Kal. Feb.   _____

2. March 11   _____   Id. Apr.   _____

3. May 17   _____   a.d. IV Non. Jun.   _____

4. July 28   _____   pr. Kal. Aug.   _____

5. September 1   _____   Non. Oct.   _____

6. November 12   _____   a.d. X Kal. Dec.   _____

GROUP ACTIVITIES

1. Measure the perimeter of the classroom in standard feet, and then approximate these measurements in Roman feet. (Round off your results to the nearest foot.)

2. Look up the distance between two cities in your state. Approximate the distance to the nearest mile, kilometer, and Roman mile.

CHAPTER 15: LEISURE ACTIVITIES

ROMANS AND THEIR LEISURE TIME

It is not surprising that the wealthy elite had more time to engage in leisure activities than almost any other group of Romans. While some participated in all manner of leisure activities, including drinking and gambling, or frequenting wild parties and brothels, others pursued more dignified and socially acceptable pastimes, such as writing, hunting, traveling, and attending cultural events.

American Academy in Rome, Photographic Archive
Fig. 65.
A circular game board has been carved into a paving stone.

Working-class people, understandably, had less time for leisure than their wealthy counterparts, but many of the same choices of leisure activities were available to them. The urban unemployed or under-employed poor, on the other hand, had more time but less money to fill their idle hours. Besides the traditional inexpensive pastimes, such as board games and ball playing, they looked forward to attending the free public spectacles and events that were often devised to keep them occupied and amused.

Slaves, of course, had almost no leisure time. And children, when they were not in school or working in their family's business, played with toys and games.

DICE, KNUCKLEBONES, AND GAMBLING

Gambling was a popular pastime for Roman adults, male and female, rich and poor. The most common gambling activity involved dice or knucklebones, which were shaken in a cup and rolled out onto a table or the ground. Roman dice were six-sided and resembled ours. Knucklebones were the actual knuckles of animals such as sheep or goats, but they were also fashioned from materials such as ivory, wood, metal, stone, glass, terracotta, and precious gems. Knucklebones were rectangular in shape. Unlike dice, they had only four usable faces with values of 1, 3, 4, and 6. Dice were generally thrown three at a time, whereas knucklebones were thrown four at a time.

Ancient sources provide the names of various throws in games played with knucklebones. We know, for example, that the worst throw (four ones) was called a "dog throw," any throw with a six was called, not surprisingly, a "six throw," four of the same value was called "vultures," and the best, when all four sides were different, was the "Venus throw."

Excessive gaming for money was looked upon askance by many Romans. In fact, during the stricter times of the Republic, gambling was forbidden, under penalty of heavy fines, except during the celebration of the Saturnalia in December. Evidence suggests, however, that, despite the laws against gambling,

Romans continued to play games of chance for money in private settings. In all probability the prosecution of gamblers became lax during the Empire. Interestingly, no such restriction was ever placed on betting at horse races or at gladiatorial shows.

Fig. 66.
A grid-shaped game board has been carved into the steps of the Basilica Julia in the Roman Forum, probably used to play *latrunculi*.

Fig. 67.
A circular carving with the word *"oraculo"* is in the Roman Forum and was perhaps used as a fortune telling game.

BOARD GAMES

Evidence that Romans played board games survives in literature and art, but perhaps nothing is more convincing than to see the abundant remains of actual ancient game boards scratched into the surface of Roman streets and buildings. No fewer than three different types of games are visible today, carved into the steps flanking the Basilica Julia in the Roman Forum. Although no definitive sets of rules have come down to us, by comparing references in literature with visual representations of Romans engaged in play and, sometimes, by studying games that are still played today, we can reconstruct or approximate these ancient pastimes.

Strategy and capture appear to have been the dominant themes in Roman board games. One of the most popular was called *latrunculi*. Although the size of the game board varies, most commonly a *latrunculi* board consisted of a grid measuring twelve squares by eight. Each player had two types of playing pieces, plain pieces and a special piece, sometimes called a "general" or a "king." The object of the game was to set up playing pieces strategically and capture the opponent's general.

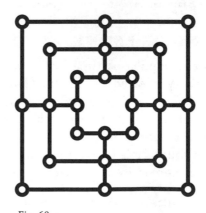

Fig. 68.
A computer generated *mola* board is shown here.

A similar game, on a smaller scale, was *mola* or "mill," a strategy game played on a board consisting of three concentric squares. Each of two players began by taking turns in placing nine pieces (usually stones or coins) on the playing board. Once the pieces were set, players took turns moving their pieces. As in *latrunculi*, the object was to capture the opponent's pieces. This was accomplished each time a player successfully created a "mill" or three pieces in a row.

Romans played many types of board games, including *duodecim scripta* (twelve lines) and *tabula*, which resembles backgammon.

COMPETITIVE SPORTS AND EXERCISE

Recreational sports and physical activity were popular pastimes for the Romans. Young men of the upper classes customarily competed in horseback riding and in contests proving skill in the use of weapons. Swimming was popular for all classes of people, as well as field sports, wrestling, and running. Comparatively little is known about women's participation in sports, although mosaics dating from the fourth century CE in Sicily depict women exercising with a ball and with hand weights.

HUNTING

Hunting was an expensive and elaborate endeavor involving dogs, horses, and large numbers of slaves as beaters and net holders. Wealthy Romans traditionally invited guests to their country estates to participate in a hunt. Sometimes, all the guests were expected to do was to wait near the nets until the prey, most often deer or wild boar, were driven into them. At that point, the trapped animals were killed by the waiting "hunters."

BALL GAMES

Roman boys and girls, men and, probably, women played ball. Balls were made of sewn leather stuffed with bits of wool and cloth. Heavier balls, like medicine balls, were weighted with sand. They came in all sizes and weights and were used to play a variety of games. Romans played ball in large, open spaces, sometimes part of bath complexes, and in smaller ball courts.

Standard Roman ball games resembled handball and team sports such as football, rugby, and soccer. Perhaps the most popular ball game was *harpastum*, which was played with a ball similar in size and density to a softball. Although we cannot be certain how *harpastum* was played, it appears to have been a rough and fast-paced team sport, resembling soccer and played on a rectangular field.

Nor do we know the specific rules for the popular ball game known as *trigon*. It involved three players who stood an equal distance apart at the points of a triangle. More than one small, hard ball was in play at a time. Strategy and quick action were used to force a player to catch or not to catch a thrown ball. The game involved feinting and left-handed throwing. Several attempts have been made to reconstruct the rules.

CHILDREN'S TOYS AND GAMES

Children's toys included jointed dolls, tops, toy animals, carts, and hoops. Children rode on swings, flew kites, played ball, and skipped stones on the surface of water. They reveled in simple games of skill, such as tossing nuts into narrow-necked jars. They built toy houses, hitched mice to small carts, rode on hobbyhorses, and flipped coins (called "heads and ships" rather than "heads or tails").

FINGER GAMES

One of the most popular games, requiring no extra equipment except a sharp mind and the ability to add quickly, was the game known as *morra*. The Romans used a Latin phrase that means 'to flash with your fingers' (*micare digitis*) to describe the action during play.

Usually played by two people, both players show any number of fingers of one hand at the same time and simultaneously call out the total number of fingers they guess will appear. If a player correctly guesses the total number of fingers shown, that person wins a point. The better the players, the faster the game.

An easier version of this game, called *par impar* (odd even) was played on the same principle, but using only combinations involving one or two fingers and guessing whether the total number of fingers shown would be odd or even.

TOURISM

The Romans were enthusiastic tourists. Although travel in the ancient world was expensive, uncomfortable, and slow, many Romans who had the time and the financial means visited remote parts of the empire. Some were able to combine travel and service, either as soldiers stationed in the outposts of provinces or as governors or bureaucrats, often accompanied by their families.

Romans made a point of seeing famous sites and places of natural beauty. Geography and travelogues were popular reading material. Not surprisingly, the great cities of Greece, especially Athens, Olympia, and Delphi and the land along the Nile River in Egypt were among the most desirable destinations. And like most tourists, Romans brought back souvenirs of their travels, especially works of art and books. Young Romans who wished to pursue higher education traveled to Athens or Rhodes to study oratory and philosophy with illustrious Greek masters.

BATHING

In the early Republic, frequenting the baths was a luxury for the wealthy, but in the Empire large-scale, public baths, called *balneae* or *thermae* were accessible free of charge or at a nominal fee to almost everyone. The larger complexes were bustling, crowded, and noisy places where Romans of all classes bathed, exercised, and socialized with friends and acquaintances. Although it has not been proven, some scholars believe that women and men generally bathed separately.

Roman bathing establishments varied in size, but they shared some common features. There was an *apodyterium*, a changing room not unlike a modern locker room, where bathers disrobed and deposited their clothes in a cubby, leaving an attendant slave to stay behind to guard their belongings.

Typically, bathers were rubbed with oil, and then they proceeded to the exercise area, the *palaestra*, where they engaged in wrestling, ball games, or other strenuous physical activity. Following this, grit, sweat, dirt, and the previously applied olive oil were scraped from their body with a curved implement called a *strigil*. Next they proceeded to the bathing pools.

Bathers first entered the *tepidarium*, the warm bath. From there they normally chose to enter the *caldarium*, the hot bath. After a return to the *tepidarium*, they might choose to take a plunge in the *frigidarium*, the cold bath. Since Romans did not believe that it was healthy to shock the body with extremes in temperature, they reentered the *tepidarium* before taking a cold plunge.

Roman baths were efficiently heated by means of a furnace or *hypocaustum* located below the bathhouse floor. Heated air rose through vents in the terracotta tiles to heat both the floors and the walls of the chambers. Slaves worked in the hot underground chambers to stoke the fires in the furnace beneath the baths.

Additional services, such as massages and hair tweezing, were also available to bathers at bathhouses. Some bathhouses were even equipped with libraries and offered cultural events such as poetry recitals, musical performances, and lectures on philosophy.

Chapter 15 Exercises: *Leisure Activities*

MATCHING COLUMNS

Match the letter of the entry in second column with the correct answer in the first column.

1. _____ *mola*   a) all ones
2. _____ Venus throw   b) choices in coin flipping
3. _____ *trigon*   c) ball game played resembling soccer
4. _____ *latrunculi*   d) to flash with one's fingers
5. _____ *micare digitis* e) board game played on three concentric squares
6. _____ heads and ships f) the values on knucklebones
7. _____ 1, 3, 4, 6   g) fast-paced ball game with three players
8. _____ *par impar*   h) odds or evens
9. _____ *harpastum*   i) played on board resembling a checker board
10. _____ dog throw   j) four different sides

FILL IN THE BLANKS

Use the following word bank to fill in the blanks:

caldarium	*hypocaustum*	olive oil
palaestra	*tepidarium*	*frigidarium*
trigon	*strigil*	*apodyterium*

Marcus and Quintus go to the Baths

It is a hot, summer day in Rome. Two brothers, Marcus and Quintus, and their paedagogus, Dares, are standing in the atrium, about to leave their house. They are on their way to a small bathhouse in their neighborhood.

Dares: Come along, you two. It's nearly the sixth hour. The day will be half over before you get to the bathhouse.

Marcus: Don't worry, we're coming.

Quintus: Wait! I forgot my ball. I promised my friend Sextus that we would play _____ with him after we bathe. I have been practicing my left-handed throw!

Quintus finds his ball, and the three hurry down the narrow street. Finally they arrive at the bathhouse. The boys pay their admission and enter the first room, the _____, where they remove their clothes and place them in a cubby.

Marcus: Be sure to keep a close watch on our clothing, Dares. A friend of mine had his toga stolen here just last week.

Quintus: Hurry up and finish applying that oil, Marcus! I see Sextus waiting for us in the _____. I can't wait to play ball!

Marcus: After the ball game, let's have a wrestling match.

Quintus: Sure, and then let's exercise with some weights. I just hope the slave who cleans us off afterwards is not too rough.

After their games and exercises, the boys lie on a table where a slave rubs them down with more _____. Then . . .

Quintus (to slave): Ouch! Take it easy with that _____! My skin is not leather, you know! Don't you have a smoother one?

Marcus: Cut it out, Quintus. You'll survive. I am going to the _____ for my warm bath. Then I'm going to take a cold plunge in the _____. What about you?

Quintus: I am going to skip the cold plunge today. After my warm bath, I am going to roast in the _____ . I like this bathhouse because it has such a good _____. I think this is the hottest water in the whole city.

Marcus: I'll meet you in the library when you have finished bathing. There's a poetry performance there today. See you later.

SHORT ANSWERS

Answer the following questions in the space provided.

1. Why do you think the very rich and the very poor spent the most time in leisure activities?

2. What did knucklebones look like and how were they different from dice?

3. What was the ancient attitude towards gambling?

4. What clues enable us to guess how Roman games were played?

5. Name two areas of competitive sport practiced by men of the upper classes.

6. Recreational hunting in the ancient world is usually associated with the wealthy. What features of Roman recreational hunting practices made it an expensive sport?

7. From what materials were Roman balls made?

8. List some toys, games and activities enjoyed by children in ancient Rome that are similar to those enjoyed by children today.

9. What were some of the foreign cities that Roman tourists liked to visit?

10. By what two Latin names were Roman baths known in the ancient world?

11. Which of the three bathing pools was used most often by the Romans? Why?

12. How were baths heated?

13. What additional services might have been offered at bathhouses to the bathers?

GROUP ACTIVITIES

1. Draw one *mola* board for every two people in the class on pieces of paper or cardboard. Each member of the class should bring in nine playing pieces. (These may be coins, buttons, pebbles, bottle caps, etc.) Follow the rules below and conduct a *mola* tournament.

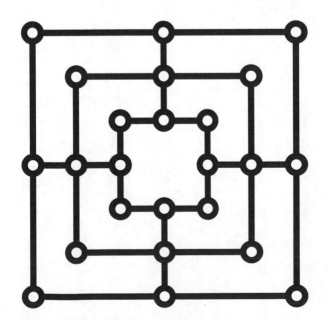

Setup

Two players alternate, placing one piece at a time on any of the circles on the playing board, until each player's nine pieces are placed. If, during setup, a player manages to place three pieces in a row (thus forming a "mill"), he or she may remove any one of the opponent's pieces from the board.

Play

Once the set up is complete, players take turns sliding their pieces along a straight line to an empty, adjacent circle. Each time a player forms a "mill" (three pieces in a row along a straight line) the player may remove one of the opponent's pieces.

A player wins when only two of the opponent's pieces are left, or when the opponent cannot move any piece.

2.   Organize a *morra* tournament in class. Here are the rules:

Two players show any combination of fingers of one hand. At the same moment that they are shown, each player shouts the total number of fingers that he or she thinks will appear. The player who correctly guesses the total number of fingers shown (the correct answer will be between two and ten) wins the point. (If both players shout the correct number at the same time, the players continue until a player wins the point). Players determine in advance how many points are needed to win.

3.   Do the games described in this chapter remind you of games that you have played? Discuss your favorite games with your classmates. Try to determine what is most appealing about these games.

Chapter 16: Public Entertainment

Games, Spectacles, and Festivals

Romans staged lavish public spectacles and events, called *ludi* or "games." Usually they were planned to coincide with certain religious festivals. Not all public spectacles, however, were termed *ludi*, but there were many varieties of *ludi*. Theatrical competitions (*ludi scaenici*) and chariot races (*ludi circenses*), for example, were actually "games," whereas gladiatorial contests and triumphal parades were not.

Three types of events were held during most of the major religious festivals. They were theatrical competitions, chariot races, and gladiatorial contests (which were often combined with wild animal hunts). In addition, victorious generals, whenever possible, chose to stage their triumphal parades during festival times.

Although we tend to associate the types of large-scale public entertainment mentioned above with the Roman Empire, most of these elaborate events evolved from simple religious rituals performed in the early days of the Republic. But Romans loved holidays and before long the calendar year was filled with religious festivals, some lasting several days.

Games and spectacles accompanied many religious festivals, but especially those in celebration of the goddesses Cybele, Ceres, and Flora, and the gods Apollo and Jupiter. The biggest and grandest festival, however, occurred in November in honor of the plebeians. The Plebeian Games, though endorsed by the state, were managed, administered, and oftentimes funded by the aediles. In this way the aediles, as elected officials, hoped to win the favor of the populace, whose votes they would need when they ran for higher office.

Fig. 69.
This ancient theater in Pompeii is frequently equipped with a temporary stage and used for performances today.

Theatrical Productions

Roman theaters were free-standing, open-air structures. Seating was arranged in a semi-circle, and an elaborate structural backdrop towered several stories above a broad, raised stage. The backdrop usually featured three doors, which were used to represent whatever buildings or houses the action of the play demanded. Musicians played in a pit in front of the stage. In some theaters canvas awnings were spread over the seating areas to protect the spectators from the sun. Theaters were used to present tragedies, comedies, mimes and pantomimes.

Tragedies and comedies were adapted from Greek originals and actors were men who wore exaggerated masks and Greek-style costumes. Plautus and Terence, who wrote in the middle years of the Republic, were two of Rome's greatest writers of comedy. Although their comedies were usually set in Greece, they contained an odd mixture of Greek and Roman cultural references.

Little survives of the most popular forms of drama: mimes and pantomimes. These were farces often based on topical and controversial political issues. Actors, wearing no masks, often impersonated and ridiculed contemporary public figures. Mime had speaking parts, while in pantomime actors relied solely on their movements, expressions, and gestures to convey their message. Both forms featured dancing and nudity. The "plots" tended to be racy and violent. One performance even included the actual execution of a criminal. Reserved and proper Romans considered mimes and pantomimes unrefined and obscene. Had they survived, mimes and pantomimes would have revealed much information about everyday life in Rome.

CHARIOT RACES

Instituted by Romulus shortly after the founding of Rome, chariot racing was arguably the oldest Roman spectator sport. In the early days, Romans sat on the slope of the Palatine hill to watch races in the valley below. Eventually the *Circus Maximus*, the largest stadium in the Roman world with a seating capacity of 250,000, was built on the site.

The racetrack of the *Circus Maximus* was oval, but the stadium itself was curved at one end and flat at the other. The flat end held 12 starting gates. Along the center of the track ran a long, thin barrier, the *spina*. At either end of the *spina* were turning posts called *metae*. It was here at the turning posts, where charioteers tried to gain crucial seconds by making tight turns, that collisions often occurred. Each race lasted seven laps, or approximately five miles. On the *spina* itself, lap counters, in the form of dolphins at one end and eggs at the other, were used to indicate the number of laps remaining in the race.

Racehorses were provided from stables owned by four companies or factions, each identified by a different color: white, blue, green, and red. Spectators cheered their favorite drivers and horses, but most of them were fans of a particular racing faction.

Fig. 70.
Above is a reconstruction of the Circus Maximus with the starting gates at the rear, left and, in the center, the *spina* with turning posts at each end.

Fig. 71.
A model of another circus without the *spina* and with the starting gates in the foreground is pictured here.

Fig. 72.
This mosaic depicts a victorious charioteer and his *quadriga,* or four-horse chariot.

American Academy in Rome, Photographic Archive

Fig. 73.
A charioteer, whip in hand, stands next to one of his horses.

To begin a race, the presiding magistrate stood in full view of the spectators and dropped a large, white cloth, called a *mappa.* Typically, charioteers, with reins tied about their waist and wearing protective helmets, drove four-horse chariots. Inscriptions, however, mention as few as three- and as many as ten-horse chariots in competition. Depending on the number of teams each faction entered, individual races consisted of four, eight, or twelve chariots. There were usually 24 races held in a day.

Charioteers were usually slaves who had everything to gain by taking risks. A successful charioteer often won not only races, but fame, wealth, and freedom.

Fig. 74.
The Flavian Amphitheater or Colosseum was expanded to include a fourth story and was richly adorned with statues in each arch.

GLADIATORIAL CONTESTS

Gladiatorial combat originated in the early practice of offering human lives to the spirits of the dead. The victims were slaves who were forced to fight to the death at the tomb of the deceased. This practice soon became a popular feature of elaborate Roman funerals. People especially looked forward to those funerals that offered the excitement of gladiatorial combat. Before long, gladiatorial contests were presented as a spectacle on their own, without a funeral, for the enjoyment of the public.

Until the late Republic, gladiatorial events were held in the Forum, the Circus Maximus, and at other places in and around Rome, sometimes in wooden or makeshift amphitheaters. Although the Colosseum was neither the first nor the only building of its type, it is certainly the most famous amphitheater in the world. Built by the Flavian emperors, the Colosseum or the Flavian Amphitheater was originally called the *amphitheatrum Caesareum*, or "the emperor's amphitheater." Because it stood next to a colossal statue of Nero, the building later became known as the Colosseum or "the place of the colossus," but it did not receive this name until the Middle Ages. The Colosseum is also referred to as an arena, a name that comes from the Latin word *harena*, meaning "sand." The floor of the Colosseum was covered with sand that was said to be pink from all the blood that was shed on it.

The Colosseum was a marvel of engineering, featuring easy access to and from seats, unobstructed views, awnings to protect the spectators from the sun, subterranean storage areas, elevators, and trap doors. Its seating capacity is estimated at about 55,000.

The spectacles in the Colosseum were an all-day affair. They traditionally began with an animal show, called a hunt, but which often included, in addition to hunting, beast fights, displays of exotic animals, performances by trained animals, and even the execution of condemned criminals who were either slain or torn apart by wild beasts. The main event of the day, however, was gladiatorial combat.

Gladiators were usually criminals, slaves (especially captured fugitives), and prisoners of war, although some free men actually chose to become gladiators. They were trained in gladiator schools to fight with different types of equipment, and most fights paired light-armed with heavy-armed gladiators. The *retiarius*, for example, was a light-armed fighter who carried only a trident, a net, and a four-pronged dagger. A *retiarius* usually fought a Samnite, who wielded a short sword and was protected by a shield, body armor, and a massive helmet.

American Academy in Rome, Photographic Archive

Fig. 75.
This frieze illustrates gladiators in training.

Audience participation was part of the excitement. A defeated gladiator could request to have his life spared. The crowd loudly voiced its approval or disapproval before an official decision was made by the person who had financed the games. If the defeated gladiator was unsuccessful in his request, he was killed and his body was removed, but only after two attendants, one dressed as Pluto and the other as Mercury, made sure that he was dead.

Winning gladiators were awarded the palm of victory and a large sum of money. The few gladiators who attained celebrity status were granted their freedom and presented with a wooden sword, indicating that they were now exempt from participating in fights to the death.

TRIUMPHAL PROCESSIONS

When a commanding general was victorious over an enemy of Rome, he had the right to request the Senate to grant him permission to celebrate his triumph. If the Senate agreed, the city prepared to receive the triumphant general and his soldiers with great festivity. Temples, shrines and statues were decorated with garlands of flowers and incense burned on the altars. The Senate, led by the magistrates, met the general, who was waiting just outside the city wall. He was dressed for the occasion in a ceremonial flowered tunic and an elaborate *toga picta* embroidered with gold. A crown of laurel wreathed his brow. He greeted the magistrates and the Senate from his triumphal chariot drawn by four horses.

The triumphal parade followed a prescribed route through the city. At the head of the procession was the Senate, followed by trumpeters, carts laden with plunder, more musicians, sacrificial animals, exotic animals, military apparatus taken from the enemy, and captives. Following the captives and preceding the general himself were lictors carrying *fasces*. (Lictors were attendants who signaled the approach of a high-ranking public official. These attendants protected the official and carried the *fasces*, a bundle of rods containing a double-headed axe. The *fasces* served as a symbol of the official's authority to bind the people and his power over life and death.) The climax of the parade, of course, was the appearance of the triumphant and resplendent general riding in his chariot, followed by his officers and his adult sons, and finally his soldiers with laurel adorning their spears. People lined the streets, throwing flowers and shouting *Io Triumphe*! (Hail, Victor!) The parade wound through the city and the Roman Forum and culminated at the statue of Jupiter in his temple on the Capitoline hill, where the general deposited his laurel wreath as an offering and where the animals were sacrificed.

Chapter 16 Exercises: *Public Entertainment*

MATCHING COLUMNS

Match the letter of the entry in the second column with the correct answer in the first column.

1. _____ Circus Maximus
2. _____ arena
3. _____ Colosseum
4. _____ *ludi scaenici*
5. _____ *retiarius*
6. _____ *Io Triumphe*
7. _____ factions
8. _____ Samnite
9. _____ *toga picta*
10. _____ *fasces*
11. _____ *mappa*
12. _____ *aedile*
13. _____ *metae*
14. _____ wooden sword
15. _____ *spina*
16. _____ lictor

a) heavily armed gladiator
b) official in charge of the Plebeian Games
c) barrier in the center of the racetrack
d) greeting for a victorious general
e) word derived from the Latin word for "sand"
f) symbol of freedom from fighting
g) turning posts on a racetrack
h) body guard
i) seating capacity of about 55,000
j) dropping it was a visual cue to start the race
k) stables that provided racehorses
l) seating capacity of about 250,000
m) theatrical events often associated with festivals
n) gladiator who carried a net
o) symbol carried by lictor
p) embroidered ceremonial toga

TRUE OR FALSE

Indicate whether each statement is true or false. If it is false, identify the error and correct it.

1. _____ *Ludi* were often staged for public entertainment during the celebration of religious festivals.

2. _____ Theatrical competitions, chariot races, gladiatorial contests and triumphal parades were all categorized as *ludi.*

3. _____ Grand public entertainment events and spectacles, performed in conjunction with religious festivals, were usually religious in origin.

4. _____ Staging the Plebeian Games in November was primarily the responsibility of the aediles.

5. _____ The stages of Roman theaters typically had a backdrop with a door through which musicians entered and left the stage.

6. _____   The most sophisticated Roman theaters were equipped with canvas awnings that could be raised or lowered to protect the spectators from the sun and the rain.

7. _____   Plautus and Terence were Roman playwrights who are believed to have invented the idea of comedy.

8. _____   Many of the most accomplished actors of the ancient world were women.

9. _____   Fortunately, the scripts of many Roman mimes and pantomimes survive to provide us with important information about life in ancient Rome.

10. _____   The Circus Maximus had a seating capacity of about a quarter of a million people.

11. _____   The shape of the Circus Maximus was a perfect oval.

12. _____   On the *spina*, the long barrier that ran down the center of the racetrack, were markers that kept a count of the number of laps the chariots made.

13. _____   The most dangerous parts of the chariot course were the turns made at the *metae*.

14. _____   Each lap of the Circus Maximus was one mile and a complete race lasted ten laps.

15. _____   There were four stables, known as factions, that provided racehorses. Fans typically cheered for a particular faction much the same way as fans at sporting events today show loyalty to a particular team.

16. _____   To begin a race, the presiding magistrate stood in full view of the spectators and dropped a large, white cloth, called a *mappa*.

17. _____   Successful charioteers, usually highly trained members of the aristocratic class, were held in great esteem by society.

18. _____   The earliest gladiators were slaves who were forced to fight to the death as an offering to the soul of the deceased at funerals.

19. _____   During the Empire, there were strict laws forbidding the staging of gladiatorial combats unless they were held as part of a funeral service.

20. _____   The Colosseum was the first building of its type in ancient Rome.

21. _____   The Colosseum was built by the Emperor Nero.

22. _____   The Colosseum could hold as many spectators as the Circus Maximus.

23. _____   Typically, gladiators were equally matched and fought with identical weapons.

24. _____   Once a gladiator was defeated in battle, death was certain.

25. _____   The prize for each victorious gladiator was a wooden sword, the symbol of victory.

26. _____   When a commanding general was victorious over an enemy of Rome, he could request that the Senate grant him permission to celebrate his triumph.

27. _____   Triumphal processions began and ended on the Capitoline hill.

28. _____ The triumphant general, wearing full military attire with a plumed helmet, was carried in his parade on the shoulders of his lieutenants.

29. _____ As the general passed through the streets, spectators threw flowers and shouted *Io Triumphe*!

30. _____ Animals were sacrificed at the conclusion of a triumphal procession.

WORD STUDY

1. **Ludus**: A *ludus* was a game or contest staged or presented to amuse or entertain the viewers. Charioteers competed in *ludi* to win races. Playwrights competed before panels of judges to win awards for the best plays. And, because a young Roman competed with his peers and was entertained by learning new things, *ludus* was also the Latin word for "school."

   What similarities can you find among the following English derivatives of the word *ludus*?

   ludicrous

   interlude

   collusion

   delusion

   illusion

   elude

2. **Theater and Amphitheater:** The English word "theater" comes to us through Latin from the Greek word *theasthai,* meaning "to see" or "to watch." A theater was a building specifically designed for seeing or watching a show, usually a play. The shape of an ancient theater was a semicircle, with the viewers seated in a curve facing the flat stage before them.

   The prefix "*amphi-*" also comes from Greek and means "both" or "around." If we place two semicircular theaters back-to-back or stage-to-stage, the shape becomes a circle, an amphitheater, a theater on both sides. The Greek prefix "*amphi-*" became the Latin "*ambi.*"

   What similarities can you find among the following English derivatives of the Greek "*amphi-*" or the Latin "*ambi-*?"

   amphibian

   ambidextrous

   ambivalence

3. **Circus Maximus:** The word "circus" comes from the Greek word *kirkos,* a circle. And a circus is a ring-shaped area for contests and performances. The largest circus in the ancient world was the Circus Maximus. In the late 18th century, the word "circus" was applied to traveling shows featuring animals and daredevil performers. These shows were performed in a tent that had a ring in the center where the action took place. Eventually some traveling shows became so large that they were known as "three-ring circuses."

    Explain what the following words have to do with a circle.

    circuit

    circuitous

    circumspect

    circumference

4. **Mime and Pantomime:** The word "mime" comes from the Greek word *mimos,* an imitator. A mime was the name of both the type of performance and the actor himself. And so a mime (the actor) performed a mime (the type of performance). In imitating another person or character, a mime relied primarily on actions and gestures, although he sometimes used words and sounds.

    A pantomime, on the other hand, traditionally used no sounds or words in his imitation. The Greek prefix *pant* means "of all." And so a pantomime was "an imitator of all."

    Explain the meaning of the following words derived from *mimos* or *pan* (all).

    mimic

    mimeograph

    panacea

    panorama

5. *Fasces*

    The *fasces,* a bundle of rods containing a double-headed axe, were carried by lictors. *Fasces* symbolized the power and authority of public officials over the people. This symbol, often depicted in ancient art, was revived in the early decades of the twentieth century when Mussolini assumed control of Italy. His movement was called "fascism" and his rule was characterized by strong governmental control over the people.

    What does the English word "fascicle" mean and how is it related to the *fasces*?

FOR DISCUSSION

1. What sort of theatrical competitions are held today? Are you aware of any dramatic performances or reenactments associated with religious holidays or festivals?

2. Research the seating capacity of large sports arenas today. How many can hold 250,000 spectators?

3. Chariot races were dangerous for the participants. Collisions occurred frequently. What kind of races or competitions that exist today can rival the experience of watching a chariot race?

4. Why do you think it was more exciting for the ancient Romans to watch gladiatorial combat between fighters with different kinds of weapons and armor?

5. Have you ever seen a "ticker-tape" parade? Research who has received this honor in American history and compare and contrast a famous "ticker-tape" parade with a triumphal procession.

CHAPTER 17: RELIGION

BASIC BELIEFS

The earliest Romans were farmers who believed that gods and spirits inhabited all living things. Gods and spirits dwelt among and around them in birds and snakes, in trees and flowers, in rivers and the wind. Knowing the names and personalities of these beings was of no consequence to these very early Romans, but securing their protection was of the utmost concern. For these divinities guided the lives of the Romans and were responsible for their prosperity or their hardships.

Romans felt obliged to acknowledge their debt to the gods—to show their appreciation to them in good times and to placate them in bad. The Roman attitude towards religion can be summed up with the Latin words *Do ut des* ("I give so that you give"). For the Romans, religion was a give-and-take arrangement, a bargain, a deal. If mortals kept their part of the bargain and did everything the gods expected them to do, the gods would reward them with protection and prosperity. What did the gods expect? The Romans believed that their gods responded favorably to formal and consistent behavior. And so Roman religion dictated the performance of specific and precise formalities called rites that were often performed at religious ceremonies.

RITES AND CEREMONIES

A rite is a sequence of actions, gestures, and words performed or spoken according to a predetermined procedure. Romans generally performed rites outdoors and with their head covered. If anything went wrong with the performance, such as a mistake or a disruption, it was necessary to begin again. A rite or a series of rites was often performed at a ceremony. The marriage ceremony, for example, included the performance of several rites, such as the recitation of the marriage vows and the sacrifice of the sheep.

Fig. 76.
A bull is about to be sacrificed under the supervision of the man with the toga pulled over his head.

OFFERINGS AND ANIMAL SACRIFICES

The Romans customarily made offerings of food and wine to gods and spirits. These offerings were either left on altars or, in the case of wine, poured into the ground. Sacred cakes, known as *mola salsa* and made from a special mixture of grain, salt, and water were prepared by the Vestal Virgins for private use in sacrifices to the household gods and in public animal sacrifices.

Although the ritualistic steps involved in sacrificing animals offered to the gods could vary, certain elements were traditional. Animal sacrifices were conducted in the open air, usually at an altar located in the consecrated

Fig. 77.
This relief depicts three animals frequently sacrificed to the gods: a bull, a sheep, and a pig.

area in front of a temple. (The interiors of temples were considered dwelling places of gods and were not used to hold ceremonies.) Before an assembled group of people, the person in charge of conducting the sacrifice stood with head covered near a fire that had been started at sunrise. A priest announced the purpose of the sacrifice or what was expected in return for the god's acceptance of the gift. The *mola salsa* was rubbed on the animal's back, its forehead was sprinkled with wine, and its spine was stroked with the sacrificial knife. It was important that the animal was a willing victim and showed no resistance. The priest spoke to the animal and explained what was about to happen. The animal's reaction to the wine, the knife, and the explanation was observed and interpreted.

The animal was killed by a specially trained person with a quick and deadly blow of an axe to its spine, and its throat was slit. Blood was collected and poured on the altar. Then the carcass was cut open and the organs, especially the liver, were examined for signs or omens and placed in the fire. If everything seemed auspicious, the gods were thought to have accepted the sacrifice. The inedible parts of the animal were then burned in the fire, and the meat was cooked and shared with the attendees.

Only domesticated animals were sacrificed, and certain kinds of animals were sacrificed to certain gods. Black animals, such as goats and sheep, were sacrificed to gods of the Underworld, for example, and Aesculapius, the god of healing, was believed to prefer roosters.

HOUSEHOLD AND FAMILY GODS

Of special importance to the Romans were the household gods, a system of divinities who inhabited nearly every part of the home. Every family had its own set of guardian spirits known as the *lares* and *penates*, who protected the individuals in the family and kept their storerooms well stocked. And there were other household gods and spirits who protected, for example, the door, the threshold, the hinges, the hearth, and the garden. It was customary for Romans to have a well-tended shrine dedicated to their *lares* in the atrium, the reception room of the house.

Fig. 78.
A *paterfamilias* is making a sacrifice to the spirits that protect his family, represented here by two dancing Lares and a snake.

RELIGION DURING THE MONARCHY

According to Roman tradition, Numa, the second of the seven kings, began the task of clarifying and organizing Roman religious practices. He is attributed with, among other things, assigning set times for celebrating religious festivals and establishing groups or "colleges" of priests to oversee the performance of rituals and ceremonies.

As Roman religion began to take shape under the Monarchy, individual gods, particularly Jupiter, Juno, and Minerva, gained importance and were worshiped together on the Capitoline Hill. Many of the strictly Roman gods and goddesses were blended and merged with the gods of other people with whom the Romans came into contact as their culture grew and developed. The Greeks, the Etruscans, and other Latin tribes were neighbors of the Romans who greatly influenced their emerging religion and their religious practices. In the East, the Greek names of gods and goddesses were well established. And so, most of the major Roman deities are associated with Greek counterparts.

RELIGION DURING THE REPUBLIC

As Rome's power continued to grow and expand beyond the confines of Italy, Romans were exposed to more and more gods and religious beliefs. Just as the Romans "romanized" foreigners in their society, so they readily adopted and "romanized" foreign gods in their religion. During the Republic, the goddesses Cybele and Isis, for example, came to Rome from the East, and Aesculapius was imported from Greece.

RELIGION DURING THE EMPIRE

Perhaps the most significant change in religious practices during the Empire was the deification of Roman rulers. Although worshiping deceased emperors and their wives as gods and goddesses at first met with large-scale resistance among the Romans, eventually rulers were declared gods and worshiped as such even before their death.

Traditionally tolerant of and indeed interested in the religious beliefs of others, by making the worship of the cult of the emperor mandatory, the Romans increased religious friction between themselves and the growing number of Christians living in the Roman Empire. The steadfast refusal of Christians to worship pagan gods, especially living emperors, resulted in Roman persecution of this religious sect. Their failure to worship the emperor caused them to be viewed as a threat to the welfare of Rome. It was not until the reign of the emperor Constantine in the late Empire that emperor worship ceased and harmony, at least for a time, was achieved with the Christians.

THE *PONTIFEX MAXIMUS*, VESTALS, AND AUGURS

In ancient Rome there was no separation between church and state and every citizen of Rome was expected to serve, when possible, in a religious capacity. Every *paterfamilias* and every elected official had religious responsibilities. Priests were chosen by their peers. The *Pontifex Maximus* was the highest priest who regulated and coordinated the activities of several priesthoods. The *Pontifex Maximus* held his office for life. During the Empire the emperor himself assumed the duties of the *Pontifex Maximus*.

Fig. 79.
The remains of the small, round Temple of Vesta, where the Vestal Virgins tended the eternal flame of Rome, are in the Forum.

Fig. 80.
The Vestal Virgins lived together around this lovely courtyard in the midst of the Roman Forum itself.

Vestal Virgins, generally six in number, administered the cult of Vesta, goddess of the hearth, in the round temple dedicated to her in the Roman Forum. Their tasks included tending the eternal flame of Vesta and preparing the special sacrificial cakes, *mola salsa*. They also were the guardians of personal wills. Vestal Virgins were given preferential treatment and were seated at places of honor at all public festivals, games, and banquets.

Vestals were recruited from patrician families when they were young children between the ages of six and ten. Requirements were clear. They had to be physically perfect and free of any marks or blemishes. Their parents had to be living at the time they were selected and had to have been married by the *confarreatio* marriage ceremony. It was a great honor for a family to have a child selected to be a Vestal Virgin.

A new Vestal was trained for ten years, served for ten years, and dedicated another ten years to training the novices. After her 30-year term was complete, she could retire and marry if she wished. Since Vestals occupied such a high place in Roman society and were allowed to own property in their own right, few chose to leave the order. Vestals dressed as a bride as a reminder of their virginity. If a Vestal violated her vow of chastity, her lover was found and whipped to death, and she was given a lamp and a loaf of bread and sealed in an underground vault.

Augurs were almost as important as the pontiffs. They were skilled in reading signs, especially those in nature, to predict the future. Signs included such things as the behavior of animals, the occurrence of thunder or lightning, and any unusual observation regarding the entrails of a sacrificed victim. If the augurs decided that the signs were not favorable, planned public and private events could not take place.

MAJOR ROMAN GODS AND GODDESSES AND THEIR GREEK NAMES

Roman Name	Greek Name	Function
Jupiter	Zeus	King of the Gods
Juno	Hera	Queen of the Gods
Minerva	Athena	Wisdom, War
Apollo	(Phoebus) Apollo	Sun, Archery, Music, Medicine, Prophecy
Diana	Artemis	Moon, Hunting, Women
Mercury	Hermes	Messenger
Mars	Ares	War
Venus	Aphrodite	Love, Beauty
Cupid (Amor)	Eros	Love, Desire
Neptune	Poseidon	Sea
Vulcan	Hephacstus	Fire, Forge
Bacchus	Dionysus	Wine
Pluto	Hades	Underworld
Ceres	Demeter	Grain, Crops
Aesculapius	Asclepius	Healing

Chapter 17 Exercises: *Religion*

SHORT ANSWERS

Answer the following questions in the space provided.

1. Explain the meaning of the Latin expression *Do ut des*.

2. What sort of behavior did the Romans believe their gods expected from them?

3. What is a rite?

4. What is a ceremony?

5. What sorts of offerings did the Romans make to their gods?

6. List several traditional features of animal sacrifices.

7. What type of animals was sacrificed?

8. What two groups of gods were collectively known as household gods?

9. What measures did Numa, the second king of Rome, take to organize Roman religious practice?

10. Name some of the non-Roman peoples who influenced the development of Roman religion and religious practices.

11. Name three eastern gods or goddesses who were imported to Rome during the Republic and "romanized."

12. What significant change in Roman religious practices during the Empire caused friction with the Christians, and why?

13. Besides tending to the eternal fire of Rome, what were two other responsibilities of Vestals?

14. What were some of the prerequisites for becoming a Vestal Virgin?

15. What punishment was inflicted on a Vestal Virgin who broke her vow of chastity?

16. Who were augurs and what did they do?

WHO AM I?

Identify the Roman god or goddess described in the blank.

1. I am handsome and powerful. On my shoulders I carry two stringed instruments, a bow and a lyre. I can shoot and I can play. I was born on the Greek island of Delos; my favorite shrine, where the oracle tells the future, is at Delphi. My twin sister is Diana. _____

2. I work all day making weapons for gods and heroes. My work is beautiful, my wife is beautiful, but I am not. I am crippled and my face is hideous to behold. Who said gods are always happy? _____

3. Yes, yes, I'm on my way! The King is forever sending me on messages. Just when I think I can take a rest, I have to strap on my winged sandals, put on my winged helmet, and take off for faraway lands to deliver information to mortals. What a life! _____

4. I am amazingly smart! Probably that has something to do with my strange birth. I sprang from Jupiter's head, full-grown and fully armed. I like to wear a war helmet and carry my shield, even when I am wearing a dress. _____

5. Have you seen my daughter? She is the sweetest, kindest, and most beautiful daughter a mother could have. I will never forgive the King of the Underworld for stealing her away. We made a bargain that he could have her for half of the year and then she would return to me. When she is gone, a chill settles on the earth and I am so distracted that I neglect my chores. Nothing grows when she is away. _____

6. Why does everyone pay so much attention to my brother, the ruler of Mt. Olympus? After all, my home in the sea is vast. I have the power to swallow up ships if I choose. I like to spend time gliding around in my underwater chariot. My trident comes in handy if I have to push sea creatures out of my way. _____

7. I love the moon. There is nothing better than walking through the woods on a bright, moonlit night. I like the moon so much that I often wear a crown with a little crescent shape. I love to run and hunt and swim. I am very pleased with my life. _____

8. It isn't easy being the King of the Gods. I am never sure just whom I can trust. I have even caught my wife trying to trick me several times. I especially have to keep my eyes on those mortals on Earth. But if they do anything to displease me, I hurl a thunderbolt at them to remind them who's the boss. _____

9. Aren't I incredibly beautiful? Mortals and gods alike practically swoon at the sight of me. My favorite season is spring. The world is so beautiful then. Animals mate and mortals fall in love. _____

10. Hiccup! Excuse me, please. I just can't seem to get enough of this sweet wine. Grapes are my favorite fruit. I wear clusters of them in my ivy crown. But what I like even better than grapes is a good, tall, goblet of full, rich wine. _____

11. It is so dark and lonely down here. How did I get stuck with this job? All day long the only sound I hear is wailing and crying. Nobody wants to be here, and neither do I! _____

12. He loves her, she loves him not. Gold-tipped arrow, lead-tipped arrow. That's the story of my life. I am a mischief-maker. I walk around on Earth and decide who should fall in love with whom, and then I shoot them with my little bow and arrows. My mother approves of my work. _____

13. That husband of mine thinks he's so great just because he is the ruler of Mt. Olympus. Sometimes I don't think he knows how lucky he is to have me as his queen. If only he would listen to me, then I wouldn't have to arrange things behind his back. _____

14. People often wonder why I carry a snake on my staff. When snakes shed their skin, they look shiny and new again, as if they had been reborn. In a way, that's what I do when I cure mortals of their illnesses. Like snakes who have shed their skin, they seem healthy and young once again. _____

15. Whenever mortals are at war with each other, that's when they need me. I am a warrior and I know how to help them. Mortals should realize how important it is for them to continue to make sacrifices to me. They never know when they will need me to help them. _____

CROSSWORD PUZZLE

Each clue below is the Greek name of a god or goddess. Write the name by which each god or goddess was known in Roman mythology in the corresponding place in the puzzle.

Across

2. Dionysus
4. Athena
6. Artemis
8. Ares
9. Poseidon
10. Apollo
11. Zeus
13. Aphrodite
14. Demeter

Down

1. Hephaestus
3. Eros
5. Asclepius
7. Hera
8. Hermes
12. Hades

ACTIVITIES

1. Choose a Roman god or goddess and research stories associated with this deity. Retell your favorite story to the class.

2. Draw a picture of a god or goddess and include in your picture clues to help identify your deity. Show your picture and ask your classmates to guess who your deity is.

3. Each person in the class will research the "biography" of a particular god or goddess and assume that god's or goddess' personality. Set a timer to ring every two minutes in the classroom. Engage in at least ten different two-minute conversations with your classmates. See how many of your classmates' personas you can correctly identify, and how many of your classmates identified yours.

CHAPTER 18: STAGES IN THE LIVES OF BOYS AND MEN

INTRODUCTION

Because most of the ancient literature that survives was written by and about Roman upper-class males, we know more about this group of Romans than, for example, we know about women and plebeians, freedmen, and slaves of both genders. Great effort has been made in recent years to fill in the glaring gaps in our knowledge about the daily life of all varieties of Romans, male and female, rich and poor, city dwellers and country people. This chapter, however, will focus on what we know best: the stages of development of a Roman upper-class male from childhood to old age, although, whenever possible, it will include information about Roman males from different classes. This chapter, and the one that follows it, "Stages in the Lives of Girls and Women," will also serve to review information presented in previous chapters.

American Academy in Rome, Photographic Archive

Fig. 81.
A Roman male child dressed in toga and wearing a bulla around his neck takes part in a religious ceremony surrounded by his family members.

CHILDHOOD CAREGIVERS

A child below the age of seven was called an *infans*, a "non-speaker." Later children were collectively known as *liberi*, a reference, perhaps, to the fact that they were "free" of responsibility. Life began for a Roman infant when his father symbolically acknowledged paternity by picking up the child laid at his feet. Soon thereafter, the baby was placed under the protection of his *paterfamilias* and his household gods and given both a name and a *bulla*.

A *bulla*, the bubble-shaped pouch made of metal, leather, or cloth, was worn around the neck as a pendant. Lucky charms or amulets were, apparently, placed inside the *bulla* to protect the child from health-related dangers and from the influence of evil spirits. Originally, only patrician children wore the *bulla*, but the practice was eventually extended to include all freeborn Roman children. *Bullae* of the children of *libertini* were made of leather. A Roman boy wore his *bulla* until his coming-of-age ceremony.

Fig. 82.
Here we see a *materfamilias* and a *paterfamilias* participating in the rituals of the cult of the *familia*.

The parents of a Roman child, when they had the financial means to do so, provided people to care for their son and to ease his transition into the *familia* and into the larger context of Roman society. The child's mother and older female siblings were probably his first teachers. In wealthier families, it was customary for a child to have several caretakers, including a wet nurse, a *paedagogus*, and tutors.

Inscriptions and references in literature suggest that not only were wetnurses, usually slaves, common in Roman households, but also that the relationship between nurse and child continued after the child was grown. In fact, inscriptions indicate that adult Roman males often felt strong sentimental attachment to their childhood nurses. In all probability, besides feeding the child, his wet nurse served as a babysitter and taught the child proper behavior.

A *paedagogus* was a male slave, usually of Greek origin, entrusted with the task of protecting especially the male children of the household from harm outside the confines of the house. They also supervised the progress of their education, presumably under the watchful eye of the father. As was true regarding nurses, the bond of Roman children to their *paedagogus* continued into later life, despite the fact that many *paedagogi* could be hard taskmasters. The role of the *paedagogus* included accompanying the child to and from school (should he be educated outside the home), assisting the child with learning his lessons, and training the child for moral and educational excellence.

SCHOOLING

Privileged Roman boys had many educational opportunities available to them. Many followed all the steps from elementary school to grammar school, to advanced training in rhetoric, completing their education in their late teens or early twenties. Less financially secure children may not have had the luxury of well-trained slaves to teach and coach them, but often their fathers took an active role in their educational instruction or paid to send their son to school. Some young boys worked as apprentices and learned a trade. Often their master at work, by serving as both guardian and teacher, supplemented the role of their father.

FROM *TOGA PRAETEXTA* TO *TOGA VIRILIS*

Roman boys played and relaxed in a *tunica,* a loose-fitting, woven, woolen garment that was sewn from two simple rectangular pieces. The *tunica* was calf-length and was worn belted. For more formal occasions, however, Roman boys wore the *toga praetexta* on top of their *tunica*. This type of toga, characterized by a small purple border around the edge, was a distinctive mark of childhood. But children were not the only ones who wore the *toga praetexta*. The highest magistrates also wore it. Both of these groups of people, children and important magistrates needed protection: children because they were prone to danger from such threats as childhood diseases, and magistrates because their welfare was closely linked to the welfare of the state. Symbolically, the border around the toga protected the person inside.

A freeborn Roman boy wore the *toga praetexta* until he reached manhood, at which time he was presented with the *toga virilis*, also called a *toga pura* or a *toga civilis*. This was a plain toga, off-white in color, made from unbleached wool.

PHYSICAL TRAINING

The pre-teen and early teenage years of a wealthy Roman boy were a period of increased physical and intellectual growth. His mother and nurse encouraged their boy to study hard and behave well. His father and *paedagogus* continued to teach him and help him perfect his command of both Latin and Greek. His father especially urged him to exercise and to spend time with his peers in such activities as ball playing, wrestling, boxing, and swimming. Often a father himself taught his son how to use weapons and how to ride a horse. Children from the lower classes, provided they were not apprenticed and at work every day, engaged in many of the same activities, but might not have had access to a horse or military weapons.

THE IN-BETWEEN YEARS

For a boy, childhood ended with his coming-of-age ceremony, usually when he was about 14 years old. During the next stage, from the age of about 14 to 25, he wore the clothing of a man, but remained under the watchful eye of his father and his family. A young man from a privileged family continued his studies, but also began to assume the role of an adult. He now accompanied his father on visits to friends and business associates. His father took an active role in facilitating his son's acceptance into Roman society by presenting him to important and influential men. He was not allowed in public without a chaperone or other adult supervision. When he was about 17 years old, he was expected to perform military service. An aristocratic young man usually accompanied a commander in the field and served on his staff.

For the privileged young man's counterparts in the lower classes, however, this was the time to stop formal schooling and to begin work and a career. Even so, he remained close to his family. In all likelihood he would serve as apprentice to his father, uncle, or another close relative. If he entered military service, it was as a common soldier.

ATTAINING MATURITY

During the Empire, three symbolic events marked a young man's transition to maturity. The first was his participation in the festival of the *Juvenalia*, a celebration instituted by Nero in the early years of the Empire. We have already mentioned (see page 18) that a Roman boy offered the first clippings of his beard at his coming-of-age ceremony. After that, it was customary for him to allow his soft facial hair to grow until his beard was full and stiff, and then have it ritually shaved during the celebration of the *Juvenalia*, thus marking his passage from youth to manhood.

The second event was his marriage, by which he assumed responsibility for his wife and his eventual children. During the Empire fines were imposed on men who remained unmarried after the age of 25.

The third event, for a young member of the senatorial class, was his candidacy for the first office of the *cursus honorum*, that of *quaestor*. A young man could serve as an urban or as a military *quaestor*. A candidate for an urban political office wore the *toga candida*, artificially whitened to signify his status as a candidate. If he was elected urban *quaestor*, he earned the right to enter the Senate. A military *quaestor* could hold office at the front during the early stages of military training and service.

A young man embarking on a political career completed all the steps of the *cursus honorum* as quickly as possible. From *quaestor* he normally progressed to the non-mandatory office of *aedile*, then *praetor*, and then *consul*. Each had a minimum age requirement that varied with time. The successful politician held his first consulship when he was in his early 40s. In the years between holding civil offices, he usually served as a priest or on the staff of a provincial governor, or enhanced his military career and reputation by demonstrating courage in battle. After he was elected *consul*, he vied for an assignment as governor of a province and for the chance to earn the glory of military victory and a triumphal parade in Rome.

While these opportunities were open to aristocrats and ambitious equestrians, working members of the equestrian and plebeian class engaged in business pursuits and tried to earn a comfortable living for themselves and for their families.

The Pursuits of Old Age

Although the average life expectancy for a Roman male remains the subject of guesswork, many did attain a very old age. Men were considered old when they reached their sixties and were no longer expected to perform public duties. Although a man in his sixties was exempt from military service and was no longer required to attend meetings of the Senate, many individuals continued to be active in both areas. Voting in public elections, however, was not generally permitted for those over sixty. A *paterfamilias*, on the other hand, retained his power for life, or until a court ruled that he was incompetent.

For the wealthy, old age offered opportunities for stimulating and productive leisure time. Both Cicero, in his treatise *On Old Age*, and Pliny the Younger, in several of his letters, discuss the intellectual pursuits of the elderly. They include social activities and intellectual endeavors, such as the reading and writing of philosophy and history.

Chapter 18 Exercises: *Stages in the Lives of Boys and Men*

SEQUENCING EXERCISE

Arrange the following events in the life of a hypothetical Roman aristocratic male in chronological order.

He serves in the army.

He is elected *consul.*

He wears a *toga virilis* to the Forum for the first time.

He receives the *bulla.*

He is elected *quaestor.*

His father picks him up from the floor.

He wears a *toga candida* for the first time.

He shaves his beard at the *Juvenalia.*

He is no longer permitted to vote in public elections.

He dedicates the first clippings of his beard to the household gods.

He is elected *praetor.*

He marries just in time to avoid paying a fine for being single.

He walks to school with his *paedagogus.*

DEFINITIONS

Briefly define the following terms

1. *infans* _____

2. *bulla* _____

3. *paedagogus* _____

4. *tunica* _____

5. *toga praetexta* _____

6. *toga pura* or *toga virilis* _____

7. *Juvenalia* _____

8. *toga candida* _____

9. *cursus honorum* _____

For Discussion

Compare and contrast the stages and events in the life of a Roman male with the growth and development of boys today. Be sure to include such topics as birth rites, clothing, schooling, coming of age, travel, military service, marriage, career, and old age.

CHAPTER 19: STAGES IN THE LIVES OF GIRLS AND WOMEN

INTRODUCTION

Rome was a patriarchal society. Men not only dominated the social, financial, political, and military arenas of life, but they discouraged participation by women. Women were not allowed to vote or to hold public office. Their sphere was the home and the family. Wealthy women were expected to manage the home, to dress and act virtuously, to train their daughters properly, and to provide a domestic atmosphere that was advantageous to the advancement of the *familia*. But, most important of all, they were expected to produce children. Despite the fact that they often remained in the background, many Roman women did rise to prominence. Some challenged authority, spoke in public settings, and participated in political affairs.

Thanks to the comparatively recent interest in gender studies, far more information about Roman women is available. Of that information, more survives about the lives of upper-class women than about the lower classes, the poor, and slave women. This chapter will address the life of a Roman female as she grows from a child to a woman. Like the one that precedes it, this chapter will serve as a review of information presented in previous chapters.

EXPOSURE OF GIRLS

In ancient Rome, unwanted children were exposed or abandoned, probably at designated locations. Exposure did not always result in the death of the child. In fact, children were often picked up by strangers, often slave traders. There were many reasons for this practice. Romans were ill-equipped and not well-disposed to caring for children impaired by birth defects. And the financial situation of the family often had a great deal to do with the decision to expose a child. It was due to monetary considerations that so many female children, from both rich families and poor, were exposed.

According to Roman custom, a prospective son-in-law received a dowry from his future wife's father or *paterfamilias*, a sum of money intended to help pay for the upkeep of his new wife. Dowries were expensive. The solution for a father or a *paterfamilias* of limited means or with many daughters was exposure. And poor families, so poor that a dowry was out of the question, could simply not afford female children. At least male children could be expected to earn an income. And so the practice of exposure continued, and the majority of exposed children were female.

CHILDHOOD CAREGIVERS AND SCHOOLING

A young female child from a wealthy family, having survived the threat of exposure, was placed in the care of a wet nurse. If her *paterfamilias* chose, she was educated along with her brothers and was cared for by the *paedagogus*. Her education could continue through grammar school if her *paterfamilias* were favorably disposed toward the education of girls and if she showed signs of academic promise. In all likelihood, however, she was turned over to her mother for training in the domestic arts.

DOMESTIC TRAINING

The life of a girl raised in an affluent family was sheltered. Her mother, rather than her father, was her primary teacher. A mother taught her daughter how to act properly in society, how to be gracious and graceful, and how to enhance her appearance. On a more practical level, a mother taught her daughter how to manage a household efficiently. Even relatively poor households had a few slaves. And so, by trailing her mother and following her example, a young girl learned how to manage the kitchen staff (if there was one) and plan meals. Where slaves were involved, she learned how to be assertive in giving commands.

Girls were also taught to do handwork by their mother. From a young age girls carded wool, which meant that they used special instruments to comb the fibers from tufts of wool kept at home in large baskets. Once the fibers were combed or carded in the same direction, they were twisted with a spindle into yarn. The yarn was woven into fabrics used to make clothing and household articles. Girls also learned how to sew.

TOYS AND GAMES

Girls played with dolls made of cloth, wax, clay, bone, and wood. Some dolls had jointed legs and arms. They also played ball games, games of skill, like tossing nuts into a narrow-necked jar, and games of chance, like knucklebones. In all probability, they played board games and strategy games with their brothers as well.

PUBERTY AND MARRIAGE

A Roman girl's childhood ended at puberty. Her *paterfamilias* usually arranged an advantageous marriage even before the girl reached her teenage years. When the child became a young woman biologically capable of producing children, her dowry was given and the wedding ceremony took place. Her wedding also served as her coming-of-age ceremony. It was then that she stopped wearing her *bulla* and made an offering of her childhood toys to the household gods.

THE *MATRONA*

As an adult, the new *matrona*, generally a teenager many years younger than her spouse, passed under the control of her husband and her husband's *paterfamilias*. She now put into action all the training she had received from her mother. She was expected to manage her new home efficiently, conduct herself modestly, promote her husband's social and occupational interests, and, above all, bear children. If she failed to produce children, no matter whether she or her husband was at fault, she would likely be divorced.

THE UNWED, DIVORCED, OR WIDOWED WOMAN

An unwed Roman woman usually remained under the control of her *paterfamilias*, although during the Empire it was somewhat easier for a mature woman, particularly a divorced or widowed woman, to obtain legal independence and the right to own property and possessions.

If a woman was divorced by her husband, usually because she did not produce an heir, her dowry and her property were returned to her father. Any children that she may have produced remained with her former husband. The divorced woman usually returned to live with her father or her nearest male relative. She was more likely to remarry if she were fertile and had produced several offspring.

During the Republic, a widow was discouraged from remarrying, and it was considered admirable to remain *univira*, a one-man woman. A widowed woman often became completely dependent on her male relatives or guardian. Under the emperor Augustus, however, widows under the age of 50 were required to remarry.

CLOTHING

Young girls and women wore a simple, calf-length *tunica*, belted at the waist. When they went out, they wore a second, longer garment, the *stola*, which covered their ankles. The *stola* was fastened at the shoulders and both belted and flounced. The *stola* was either a natural, undyed color or dyed bright colors with vegetable and mineral dyes. Girls and women also wore a large shawl, called a *palla*, which could cover the head as well as the body.

Women and girls used parasols to protect themselves from the sun, and fans made of feathers, bone, wood, or fabric to keep themselves cool. They wore leather shoes and sandals, some dyed and decorated.

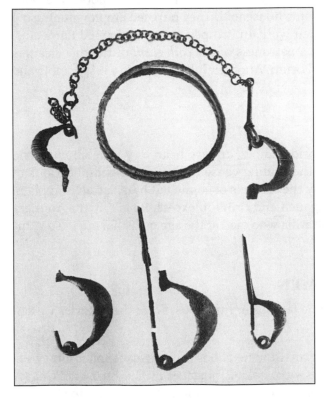

Fig. 83.
Garments were held in place by *fibulae* or pins resembling the modern safety pin. Sometimes they were plain, like these, and sometimes they were made of gold or silver and adorned with gems.

Fig. 84.
Roman women sometimes used hair extensions to enable them to wear elaborate hairdos such as the one illustrated above.

BEAUTY ENHANCEMENTS

Roman women had many beauty options available to them. Some curled their hair with curling irons and used henna to dye it red. They used hairpieces and braid extenders to make their hair thicker or longer. Roman hairstyles came in and out of fashion and ranged from the simple, close-to-the-scalp styles of the early Republic and early Empire to the piled up curls of the middle and later Empire.

Women used both perfume and makeup, made from both local and imported products. Many examples of elaborate Roman jewelry survive. Necklaces, brooches, and bracelets, made of gold or silver and set with precious and semi-precious stones abound, but perhaps the most interesting examples of adornment are crowns and earrings. Many finely worked crowns, made of sheets of gold and with pearls and stones resembling berries, survive. Earrings were often elaborate affairs with small figures and flowers fashioned in gold. The figures on the earrings were accented with gems and suspended on chains that reached the shoulders from the earlobes.

WORKING WOMEN, SLAVE WOMEN, AND FREEDWOMEN

Many women, especially the poor and the *libertinae*, worked for a living; others were slaves. Most slave women faced a life of drudgery, beatings, and exploitation. Some masters allowed slaves to form informal families, and some household slaves, such as nurses and personal attendants, enjoyed relative comfort and the promise of eventual freedom.

Those slaves who attained their freedom had the same opportunities available to poor, free-born women. Many ex-slaves married freedmen from the same household. They pursued employment using whatever skill they had, or helped their husbands in their work. In Pompeii, a woman named Eumachia, for example, rose from humble origins to be become a patroness of the *collegium* of the dry cleaners and the namesake of the largest public building in the Forum. Another, Julia Felix, ran a respectable and lucrative business, perhaps a rooming house.

OLD AGE

Women who could no longer bear children were considered old, and we hear very little about them. Many women, however, did not reach old age since the leading cause of death was complications of pregnancy and childbirth. Old women were frequently the subjects of comic but harsh attacks in plays. They are portrayed as evil crones who prey on young men and drink to excess. But Pliny the Younger tells of a cheerful old woman named Ummidia Quadratilla who died at the age of 79, having led a comfortable and pleasant life.

HISTORICAL AND LEGENDARY WOMEN

Many Roman women, legendary and historical, became famous or infamous. From their stories we can learn what traits the Romans valued in their women.

From the earliest times, the Romans struggled against the neighboring Etruscans for military supremacy. In one such struggle, several young Romans were held as hostages by the Etruscan king. A young woman named Cloelia escaped from her guards and led a small band of Roman girls to safety by swimming (some accounts say on horseback) across the Tiber River. The Romans celebrated Cloelia's courage by erecting a statue of her on the Via Sacra in the Roman Forum.

Cornelia, one of the most revered women of republican Rome, became a symbol of the ideal mother. She was the daughter of the famous general Scipio Africanus, who defeated Hannibal. Although she was still young and beautiful when she was widowed, she remained an *univira*, declining a marriage offer from the pharaoh of Egypt. This noble woman, caring little for wealth, remarked to a gathering of women who were showing off their newly acquired jewelry that, as far as she was concerned, her two young sons were her jewels.

During the political turmoil of the late Republic, Fulvia became the archetype of the wicked matron who meddled in the political realm of men. She supported the policies of her unscrupulous husband, P. Clodius Pulcher, and called for vengeance after he was murdered, focusing much of her hatred on Cicero, his most vocal enemy. She eventually married Marcus Antonius (Mark Antony), an ally of Caesar. She supported her husband's cause so strongly that she reputedly took up arms in battle against his enemy.

Chapter 19 Exercises: *Stages in the Lives of Girls and Women*

Definitions

Briefly define the following terms.

1. exposure _____

2. dowry_____

3. matrona _____

4. univira _____

5. stola _____

6. palla _____

Sequencing Exercise

Arrange the following events in the life of a hypothetical Roman aristocratic female in chronological order.

She is trained to spin wool.

She receives her *bulla*.

She falls under the authority of her husband's *paterfamilias*.

She stops wearing her *bulla*.

She is married.

True or False

Indicate whether each statement is true or false. If it is false, identify the error and correct it.

1. _____ Roman aristocratic girls were usually sent to grammar school.

2. _____ Slaves devoted many hours to carding and spinning wool and to weaving and sewing the clothes worn by their masters.

3. _____ Although we know that Roman aristocratic boys played with toys, we have no evidence to tell us about girls' toys.

4. _____ When Roman girls reached the age of seven, they stopped wearing their *bulla*.

5. _____ If a Roman matron failed to produce children, no matter whether she or her husband was at fault, she would likely be divorced.

6. _____ The children of divorced parents usually lived with their mother.

7. _____ Women and girls used parasols to protect them from the sun and fans to keep themselves cool.

8. _____ Roman women used curling irons and hairpieces to create elaborate and exotic hairdos.

9. _____ Although Roman women had the ability and the skill to run their own businesses, they were forbidden by Roman law.

10. _____ The only public statues of Roman women that survive are those of empresses or members of imperial families.

ACTIVITIES

1. From what you have learned about Roman women, write the autobiography of a virtuous Roman woman, from her birth to her old age. Include details about her early years at home, her marriage, her own family, her aspirations, and her old age.

2. Find images of Roman women, especially sculptures. Study their hairdos and create the same hairdo on a classroom volunteer.

CHAPTER 20:
RESOURCES

GENERAL WORKS ON DAILY LIFE

All of these general works were used extensively by the authors. They are also highly recommended to both teachers and students seeking further information and sources.

BOOKS

Adkins, Leslie and Roy A. *Handbook to Life in Ancient Rome.* New York and Oxford: Oxford University Press, 1994.

Carcopino, Jerome. *Daily Life in Ancient Rome.* New Haven: Yale University Press, 1960.

Dupont, Florence. *Daily Life in Ancient Rome.* Cambridge: Blackwell, 1989.

Johnston, Harold W. *The Private Life of the Romans.* New York: Scott, Foresman 1903 and 1932. Out of print but available online at http://www.forumromanum.org/life/johnston_intro.html

Matz, David. *Daily Life of the Ancient Romans.* Westport, Connecticut: Greenwood Press, 2002.

Paoli, Ugo Enrico. *Rome: Its People, Life and Customs.* Essex: Longmans Green & Co., 1963.

Robinson, O. F. *Ancient Rome: City Planning and Administration.* New York: Routledge, 1992.

Shelton, Jo-Ann. *As the Romans Did.* New York and Oxford: Oxford University Press, 1988.

Smith, William. *A Dictionary of Greek and Roman Antiquities.* London, 1875. Available online at http://penelope.uchicago.edu/Thayer/E/Roman/Texts/secondary/SMIGRA/home.html

Stambaugh, John E. *The Ancient Roman City.* Baltimore: The Johns Hopkins University Press, 1988.

WEBSITES

Vita Romana Cottidiana http://latin.austincollege.edu/latin/vitaromana/

Daily Roman Life http://www.uvm.edu/~classics/webresources/life/

Daily Life Texts http://www.personal.kent.edu/~bkharvey/roman/texts/textlife.htm

Daily Life Overhead Slides http://www.mmdtkw.org/ALRIAncRomUnit9Slides.html

BBC The Romans http://www.bbc.co.uk/history/ancient/romans/

Encyclopaedia Romana http://penelope.uchicago.edu/~grout/encyclopaedia_romana/index.html

FILMS

There are no individual films that give an accurate depiction of Roman daily life, but a large number do have scenes which can illustrate aspects of what it was like to be a Roman. They will be cited under the appropriate chapter topic. Two television mini-series come close:

A.D. The Series (Vincenzo Labella, Producer, 1984) is a six-hour mini-series that covers the years 30–69 CE and intertwines the Book of Acts from the New Testament (to which it is very faithful) with events of Roman history drawn mostly from Suetonius and Tacitus. It is well-acted and the Roman material is fairly accurate but depicts the Romans in a very negative light, since it is the story of the development of Christianity. The fictional characters, on the other hand, have adventures which bear little resemblance to reality, but the details of daily life that surround their ridiculous soap operas are well-done, especially in the scenes depicting a wedding, a slave market, street scenes, gladiator training and the great fire of 64 CE.

Rome (Bruno Heller and John Milius, Producers, HBO 2005) portrays the civil wars of Caesar and Pompey, ending with the Ides of March. It is an excellent drama with a wealth of very accurate images of daily life, but contains a great deal of sex, nudity, and violence. The current website http://www.hbo.com/rome/ contains much useful information and pictures. On the image of Rome in films in general see the following:

Cyrino, Monica Silveira. *Big Screen Rome*. New York: Blackwell, 2005.

S. Joshel, M. Malamud, and D. McGuire. *Imperial Projections: Ancient Rome in Modern Popular Culture*. Baltimore: The Johns Hopkins University Press, 2001.

Solomon, Jon. *The Ancient World in Cinema*. New Haven: Yale University Press, 2001.

Winkler, Martin (ed.). *Gladiator: Film and History*. London: Blackwell, 2004.

Wyke, Maria. *Projecting the Past*. New York: Routledge, 1997.

FICTION

There are hundreds of historical novels that focus on Rome. Many of them are both entertaining and accurate. The novels of Paul Anderson can be as effective as Caesar's Gallic Wars in attracting readers to ancient history. Although contemporary readers often assert that their works are meant to be enjoyed rather than assigned as required reading, the latter does not always preclude the former. Reading good, modern fiction about the ancient world can help students become more engaged with the subject. Older authors, such as Anderson, are only as accurate as their own times permit, and even some of the more recent authors don't bother with the realities of Roman life at all. In general see Fred Mench's website: http://loki.stockton.edu/~roman/fiction/index.htm or Stephan Cramme's list (in German) at http://www.hist-rom.de/index.html. There are however ten contemporary authors who do a very good job of storytelling and pay close attention to details. Here are seven living authors, in alphabetical order who have written continuing series based on Roman life:

Lindsey Davis writes a series of murder mysteries featuring a comic detective named M. Didius Falco who prowls the mean streets of Rome and its provinces. You can see a list of her books at: http://www.lindseydavis.co.uk/index.html

Colleen McCullough traces the end of the Republic in her *Masters of Rome* series. For details see: http://loki.stockton.edu/~roman/fiction/mccullough.htm

John Maddox Roberts is writing a series called SPQR which features an aristocratic crime solver named Decius Caecilius Mettellus and is set at the end of the Republic. For a list and summaries see: http://italian-mysteries.com/JMRap.html

Rosemary Rowe also has a detective series (*Libertus Mysteries of Roman Britain*) but it is set in Roman Gloucester, and her detective is a freedman and a mosaic-maker. http://www.raitken.wyenet.co.uk

Steven Saylor is another mystery writer in the hard-boiled detective mode featuring an aging Gordianus the Finder in a series called *Roma Sub Rosa*. His website http://stevensaylor.com/ also contains lists of other historical novels and books on the Roman world in general.

Simon Scarrow writes military page-turners set around the conquest of Britain, but they also contain many details about everyday life as well. The tale begins with *Under the Eagle*. A website can be found at http://www.scarrow.fsnet.co.uk

David Wishart has a Roman detective named Marcus Valerius Messalla Corvinus but he has also written a number of non-mystery historical novels. You can see a list at http://www.stockton.edu/~roman/fiction/wishart.htm

An individual novel that can be used to highlight Roman daily life is *A.D. 62: Pompeii* by Rebecca East (New York: iUniverse, 2003). She has a website to accompany the book (http://www.rebecca-east.com/gateway.html) that illustrates the objects, settings and even the buildings in the story. What makes it attractive to students is the science fiction premise of the tale. The heroine is a classics student who is sent back in time to gather data about Pompeii a few years before the eruption of Mt. Vesuvius. She is then trapped there when the time machine fails, and she is sold into slavery. She observes the Roman world from the point of view of a scholar and a participant, building her story on real objects, places and people. And she knows what the future holds for those around her. The first-person narrative is supposed to be her report that she has left hidden to be found by those who sent her back in time. She uses the opportunity to relate not only her adventure but also to detail what she could see as a slave in a wealthy, if dysfunctional, household.

Another novel recommended (http://www.lindseydavis.co.uk/courseofhonour.htm) is based on another dysfunctional Roman family, but it is imperial and lives on the Palatine. Lindsey Davis' only non-mystery (*The Course of Honour*, New York: Mysterious Press, 1998) is the story of Antonia Caenis, the mistress of Vespasian. As a slave and then a prosperous freedwoman, Caenis describes life from the underside, but she also rises in society with the fortunes of her lover. Through her eyes we can follow the life course of a *libertina*, albeit a fortunate one.

Finally, there is a historical thriller by Robert Harris called *Pompeii: A Novel* (New York: Random House, 2003). See http://italian-mysteries.com/RHA01.html for more information. It features an engineer in the aqueduct service named Marcus Attilius Primus who tries to determine why the water suddenly stopped flowing to Misenum. Of course we know that Vesuvius is about to erupt, but he rushes into the mouth of danger to do his job. In the process students learn a lot about engineering, geology and the nature of Roman life on the bay of Naples. Attilius is a mid-level functionary who has to deal with all elements of society and nature. The volcano is the least of his problems. Unfortunately all of these novels have some sexual content which some might find offensive.

SPECIFIC RESOURCES FOR CHAPTER TOPICS:

The following books and websites will be useful to anyone seeking more information on the topics covered in each of our chapters. The general websites above have internal and external links that cover most of these topics, but we have also included a few specialized ones. Since the WWW is constantly changing, we recommend that you try Google.com or a similar search engine to find sites. If you use the Latin terms, you can avoid some of the less reliable sites. The novels, films, and documentary videos were all available at the time of writing. The full titles of the sources listed first under each topic can be found after the author's name in the list of books on page 147. The number following each name refers to the chapter number in each book.

CHAPTER 1: ROMAN SOCIETY

DuPont 1–2; Johnston 2, 5; Shelton 1

Earl, Donald. *The Moral and Political Tradition of Rome.* London: Thames and Hudson, 1967.

Gardner, Jane F. *Being a Roman Citizen.* London: Routledge, 1993.

Taylor, David. *Roman Society.* Walton-on-Thames: Nelson, 1980.

Many of the recently published detective novels set in Rome convey an accurate image of the structures of Roman society since they feature sleuths who tend to have to work with all walks of life. Davis (*Silver Pigs*) and Saylor (*Roman Blood*) are particularly vivid in their depictions of the mean streets of Rome, and McCullough (*The First Man in Rome*) makes the struggles within the upper classes come alive. In films, the HBO series *Rome* offers a starkly realistic portrait of class divisions, but the BBC show, *Pompeii: The Last Day*, is also useful.

CHAPTER 2: THE FAMILY

DuPont 6; Johnston 1; Shelton 2

Dixon, Suzanne. *The Roman Family.* Baltimore: The John Hopkins University Press, 1992.

———. *The Roman Mother.* Norman: University of Oklahoma Press, 1988.

Bradley, Keith. *Discovering the Roman Family.* New York and Oxford: Oxford University Press, 1991.

Harris, W.V. "Child exposure in the Roman Empire." *JRS* 84 (1994): 1–22.

Rawson, Beryl. *The Family in Ancient Rome.* Ithaca: Cornell University Press, 1986.

Wiedemann, Thomas. *Adults and Children in the Roman Empire.* New Haven: Yale University Press, 1989.

Most works of fiction do not give accurate representations of the Roman family, choosing instead to be anachronistic and portray family dynamics as more modern and familiar. This is understandable since modern readers and viewers would find the inequities of the system distasteful. East and Roberts come the closest in fiction. The closest to a depiction of a *paterfamilias* in film is its satiric opposite in *A Funny Thing Happened on the Way to the Forum.*

CHAPTER 3: THE RELIGIOUS RITUALS OF THE FAMILY

Carcopino 4; Johnston 3, 12; Shelton 3

Scheid, John. *An Introduction to Roman Religion.* Indiana: Indiana University Press, 2003.

Beard, Mary and North, John and Price, Simon. *Religions of Rome.* Vol. 1, *A History.* Cambridge: Cambridge University Press, 1998.

The family rituals which frequently occur in fiction are usually too brief to be useful, but the birth of Caesarion in *Cleopatra* (1963), the wedding scene in *A.D. The Series* and the funeral scene in Davis' *Scandal Takes a Holiday* are instructive.

CHAPTER 4: ROMAN HOUSING

DuPont 4–5; Johnston 6; Shelton 4

Clarke, John. *The Houses of Roman Italy, 100 B.C.– A.D. 250: Ritual, Space and Decoration.* Berkeley: University of California Press, 1991.

Richter, G.M.A. *The Furniture of the Ancient Greeks, Etruscans, and Romans.* London: The Phaidon Press, 1966.

Wallace-Hadrill, Andrew. *Houses and Society in Pompeii and Herculaneum.* Princeton: Princeton University Press, 1994.

Davis, Saylor, and Roberts do an excellent job of describing where and how their main characters live in Rome, while East and Harris have detailed descriptions of houses and villas in the bay of Naples area. HBO's *Rome* is the best depiction of all kinds of housing and living conditions in any film about this period.

CHAPTER 5: DOMESTIC LIFE

DuPont 14–16; Johnston 7–8; Shelton 5

Sebesta, Judith Lynn and Larissa Bonfante, (eds.). *The World of Roman Costume.* Madison: University of Wisconsin Press, 1994.

Brothwell, Don and Patricia. *Food in Antiquity.* Baltimore: The Johns Hopkins University Press, 1998.

Dalby, Andrew and Sally Grainger. *The Classical Cookbook.* Los Angeles: Getty Museum, 1996.

Giacosa, Ilaria Gozzini. *A Taste of Ancient Rome.* Chicago: University of Chicago Press, 1992.

Ricotti, Eugenia Salza Prina. *Dining as a Roman Emperor.* Rome: L'Erma di Bretschneider, 1999.

The books of Davis, Saylor, Roberts, East, and Harris abound in detailed glimpses into domestic life. In films, the HBO series *Rome* offers realistic images, but the BBC show *Pompeii: The Last Day* is also useful.

CHAPTER 6: EDUCATION

Carcopino 5; Johnston 4; Shelton 6

Bonner, S. *Education in Ancient Rome.* Berkeley: University of California Press, 1977.

Hopkins, Keith. "Everyday life for the Roman schoolboy." *History Today* 43 (1993): 25–30.

 The school scenes in older or juvenile fiction are not accurate enough to recommend.

CHAPTER 7: SLAVERY

DuPont 3; Johnston 5; Shelton 8

Bradley, K. R. *Slavery and Society at Rome.* Cambridge: Cambridge University Press, 1994.

———. *Slaves and Masters in the Roman Empire: A Study in Social Control.* Oxford: Oxford University Press, 1987.

Wiedemann, Thomas. *Greek and Roman Slavery.* Baltimore: Johns Hopkins, 1981.

 Trusted household slaves abound in fiction, but East and Saylor do a good job of depicting the less pleasant aspects. East's novel, along with Davis' *Course of Honor,* and Paul Anderson's *A Slave of Catiline,* are told from a slave's point of view. That is also true for the wonderful movie *A Funny Thing Happened on the Way to the Forum.* There is a slave market scene in the films *The Robe* and *A.D. The Series,* the oppression is manifest in *Gladiator* and in *Pompeii: The Last Day,* but by far the best depictions are in *HBO's Rome.*

CHAPTER 8: FREEDMEN AND FREEDWOMEN

DuPont 3; Shelton 9

Bradley, K.R. *Slavery and Society at Rome.* Cambridge: Cambridge University Press, 1994.

Duff, A.M. *Freedmen in the Early Roman Empire.* Oxford: Oxford University Press, 1928.

Treggiari, Susan. *Roman Freedmen during the Late Republic.* Oxford: Oxford University Press, 1969.

 Davis' *Course of Honor* is the life story of a very prominent freedwoman, and the detective in Rowe's mysteries had been a slave, so they both explore the complicated relationships of patrons and clients. Films rarely even mention this status.

CHAPTER 9: URBAN LIFE

Carcopino 1; DuPont 8–9; Robinson 1–7; Shelton 4; Stambaugh 6–12

Connolly, Peter. *The Ancient City.* Oxford: Oxford University Press, 1998.

Anderson, James. *Roman Architecture and Society.* Baltimore: The Johns Hopkins University Press, 1997.

 All of the recent detective novels focus on the grittier features of Rome, but Davis (sewers, fires, baths), Saylor (crime, streets, shops), Roberts (slums, building, festivals), and East (buildings in Pompeii) have abundant and accurate detail. Harris has a wealth of detail on aqueducts and their care, and Scarrow (*The Eagle's Prophecy*) gives an out-of-towner's take on the slums. There are great images of urban living in *Sign of the Cross, A.D. The Series, Pompeii: The Last Day,* but especially in *HBO's Rome.*

CHAPTER 10: LAW AND ORDER

Robinson 12–13

Crook, J.A. *Law and Life of Rome.* Ithaca: Cornell University Press, 1967.

Nippel, Wifried. *Public Order in Ancient Rome.* Cambridge: Cambridge University Press, 1995.

There are realistic depictions of daily crime and violence in the detective novels and of course in *HBO's Rome.*

CHAPTER 11: FARMING

Shelton 7

Cato the Censor. *On Farming.* Translated by Ernest Brehaut. New York: Columbia University Press, 1933.

White, K.D. *Roman Farming.* Ithaca: Cornell University Press, 1970.

———. *Farm Equipment of the Roman World.* Cambridge: Cambridge University Press, 1975.

Other than Saylor's *Catilina's Riddle* where Gordianus tries farming and a *latifundia* scene in *Barabbas*, there is little to report.

CHAPTER 12: OCCUPATIONS

Carcopino 7; DuPont 7; Johnston 11; Shelton 7

Goldsworthy, Adrian. *The Complete Roman Army.* London: Thames and Hudson, 2003.

Williams, Brian. *Ancient Roman Jobs.* Aspects of Roman Life. Chicago: Heinemann Library, 2002.

McCullough's books are an excellent portrait of aristocratic occupations and careers. Various craftsmen frequently appear in the detective novels as background or plot devices. Rowe's is even a mosaic-maker by profession and Falco's large family includes many tradesmen and craftsmen of varying skill levels. Aristocratic careers are never depicted accurately or comprehensibly in any films, but trades do get some exposure in *A.D. The Series, Pompeii: The Last Day,* and especially in *HBO's Rome.* Military careers get excellent treatment in McCullough and Scarrow. There are some useful glimpses of warfare and military life in *Spartacus, Gladiator, Masada* and *HBO's Rome,* but the many PBS and History Channel documentaries are much more accurate.

CHAPTER 13: TRAVEL AND TRADE

Matz 5; Johnston 10; Robinson 9–10

Aldrete, G. and D. Mattingly. "Feeding the City" in D. Potter and D. Mattingly, *Life, Death, and Entertainment in the Roman Empire.* Michigan, 1999. Pages 171–204.

Hodge, Peter. *Roman Trade & Travel.* London: Longman Publishing Group, 1978.

Perrottet, T. *Pagan Holiday: On the Trail of Ancient Roman Tourists.* New York: Random House, 2003.

The only references to this topic appears in novels whose characters travel. Davis dwells more on the difficulties of travel than the others.

Chapter 14: Measuring Time and Space

DuPont 4, 10–12; Scheid 4

www.Roman-Britain.org/calendar/htm

Hannah, Robert. *Greek and Roman Calendars: Constructions of Time in the Classical World.* London: Duckworth Publishing, 2005.

Other than the occasional use of a Latin phrase or a shot of a calendar in the opening of *Rome*, fiction writers generally avoid the unfamiliar Roman systems.

Chapter 15: Leisure Activities

Carcopino 9; Johnston 9; Shelton 14

Austin, R.G. "Roman Board Games." *Greece and Rome* 4 (1934): pp. 24 & 76.

D. Balsdon, J.P.V.D. *Life and Leisure in Ancient Rome.* London: Bodley Head, 1969.

Fagan, G. *Bathing in Public in the Roman World.* Ann Arbor: University of Michigan Press, 1999.

Perrottet, T. *Pagan Holiday: On the Trail of Ancient Roman Tourists.* New York: Random House, 2003.

Baths are critical to the plots of several mysteries, and tourism is the focus of Davis' *See Delphi and Die.* Films adore bathing scenes, and just about every film we have mentioned has one. There are even authentic knucklebones used in *Sign of the Cross*, which has the most famous bath scene of all—the milk bath of Poppaea.

Chapter 16: Public Entertainment

Carcopino 8; DuPont 4; Johnston 9; Shelton 14

Bomgardner, D.L. *The Story of the Roman Amphitheater.* London and New York: Routledge, 2000.

Beacham, R. *Spectacle Entertainments of Early Imperial Rome.* New Haven: Yale University Press, 1999.

Futrell, A. *Blood in the Arena: The Spectacle of Roman Power.* Austin: University of Texas Press, 1997.

Mahoney, Anne. *Roman Sports and Spectacles.* Newburyport, MA: Focus Publishing, 2001.

Kyle, Donald. *Spectacles of Death in Ancient Rome.* London: Routledge, 1998.

Potter, D.S. and J.D. Mattingly (eds.), *Life, Death, and Entertainment in the Roman Empire.* Ann Arbor: University of Michigan Press, 1999.

Davis and Saylor treat these events in passing, whereas films revel in them. The best arena scenes are in *Sign of the Cross*, *Spartacus*, and *Gladiator*. *Ben-Hur* still has the best chariot race. There are no films that do justice to the theater or a triumph, although *Rome* comes close.

CHAPTER 17: RELIGION

Shelton 15

Adkins, Lesley and Roy A. Adkins. *Dictionary of Roman Religion.* New York: Facts on File, 1996.

Beard, Mary and North, John and Price, Simon. *Religions of Rome.* Vol. 1, *A History.* Cambridge: Cambridge University Press, 1998.

Scheid, John. *An Introduction to Roman Religion.* Indiana: Indiana University Press, 2003.

Turcan, Robert. *Cults of the Roman Empire.* London: Blackwell Publishing Ltd., 1996.

With the possible exception of *A.D. The Series* and *Rome*, writers and filmmakers either ignore or gravely misinterpret Roman religion, in spite of the numerous gods, shrines, statues, and festivals that appear in all works of fiction. None of them can be used with confidence to illustrate actual Roman beliefs and practices.

CHAPTER 18: STAGES IN THE LIVES OF BOYS AND MEN

Harlow, M. and R. Laurence. *Growing Up and Growing Old in Ancient Rome: A Life Course Approach.* London: Routledge, 2002.

The novels which are series do follow the lives of some of the minor characters through time, especially the male children of Gordianus in Saylor. They are not typical. McCullough follows her aristocratic characters through every stage of life, especially Caesar, Cicero, and Pompey, as did Robert Graves in *I, Claudius.* The TV version of the last comes close to showing Roman boys growing up.

CHAPTER 19: STAGES IN THE LIVES OF GIRLS AND WOMEN

Shelton 13

Balsdon, J.P.V.D. *Roman Women.* Westport, Connecticut: Greenwood Press, 1962.

Lefkowitz, M. and M. Fant, *Women's Life in Greece and Rome: A Source Book in Translation.* 3rd Ed. Baltimore: The Johns Hopkins University Press, 2005.

Dixon, Suzanne. *Reading Roman Women: Sources, Genres and Real Life.* London: Duckworth Publishing, 2001.

Fantham, Elaine. *Women in the Classical World.* Oxford: Oxford University Press, 1994.

Davis' *Course of Honor* is unique in tracing the life-course of a freedwoman. Women abound in the films, but none really show the life-course of a Roman girl.

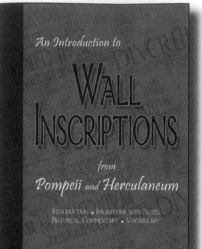

Once Upon a Tiber
An Offbeat History of Rome

Rose Williams
Mark Bennington, *Illustrator*

This lighthearted yet historically accurate history of Rome in English tells the story of the major Roman events and personalities from the founding of the city to the time of Romulus Augustulus. A pertinent Latin quote (with translation) begins each chapter, and brief notes explain which ancient author supplied the more unusual bits. A glossary of names, survey of Roman history, and index round out the features.

Designed for students studying Latin, this history covers all the pertinent facts but adds a mite of salty wit to make the facts a bit more digestible. Williams is especially good at pointing out the ironies and foibles of the mighty Romans and noting the oddities that dotted their history. Here you will find the true facts about Venus the Bald and Marius the Muddy as the ancient writers recorded them. The lives of major Roman authors are also included, and even they do not escape the lens of Williams' wit.

Features:

- 29 chapters in English, averaging 4 pages each
- Line illustrations by Mark Bennington throughout
- Brief notes to the chapters
- Glossary of names and terms
- Index

viii + 134 pp (2002) paperback, ISBN 1-898855-78-1

The Comic History of Rome

Gilbert Abbott À Beckett
John Leech, *Illustrator*

Beckett's *The Comic History of Rome*, first published in London in 1852, is now available in a reprint. The author's intent is to combine **instruction** with **amusement**. Teachers and students alike will welcome Beckett's humor and often satiric representation of the great chapters of Roman history from the earliest times to the death of Caesar. Witty satire against some of most well known Roman historical figures and illustrations that frequently are comic in nature will bring a smile to the reader of this unique history.

100+ illustrations, xii, 308 p. (1852, rp t. 1996), Paperback, ISBN: 978-0-86516-333-1

Bolchazy-Carducci Publishers, Inc.
www.BOLCHAZY.com

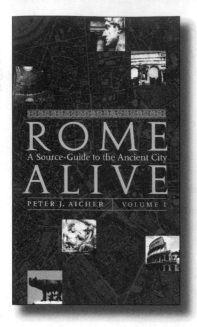

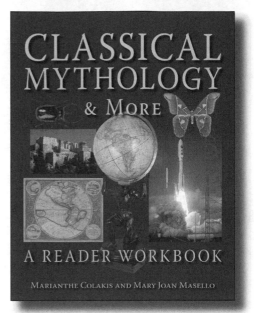

CLASSICAL MYTHOLOGY AND MORE: *A READER WORKBOOK*

Marianthe Colakis and Mary Joan Masello

This engaging workbook is an unparallelled classical mythology resource for middle- and high-school aged students. Students in Latin, English, and Language Arts classes will enjoy and learn from these fresh retellings of timeless tales from Hesiod, Homer, Ovid, and other ancient authors. Creation myths, stories of the Titans and Olympians, legends of the Trojan War cycle, love stories, and tales of transformation are all included here. Numerous illustrations and a wide variety of exercises, reflections, and vocabulary enrichment tasks accompany each myth chapter. Students preparing for the ACL Medusa Myth Exam, the ACL National Mythology Exam, or local, state, or national certamen competitions will find in this an indispensable tool.

Features: • Fresh retellings of favorite myths, based on primary Latin and Greek sources • Numerous illustrations show myth's influence on art, science, popular culture • Sidebar summaries keep the reader oriented and engaged • Maps illustrating routes of heros and key locations and genealogical charts • Varied exercises at the end of each chapter • Quirky and fun information about English words derived from the myths • Reflections upon the enduring quality and influence of the myths • Glossary of names and places, arranged chapter by chapter for quick review, with a pronunciation guide • Bibliography for further reading and index

(2007) 8½" x 11" paperback, ISBN 978-0-86516-573-1

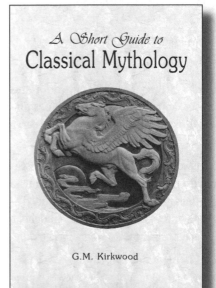

A SHORT GUIDE TO CLASSICAL MYTHOLOGY

G. M. Kirkwood

A Short Guide to Classical Mythology is a concise reference for general readers, tudents, and teachers. Kirkwood's treatment of the characters, settings, and stories of ancient mythology emphasizes their importance in Western literature. The entries are ordered alphabetically and vary in length according to their significance.

Features:

• Complete reference list with pronunciations
• Principal stories of classical mythology
• Emphasis on literary importance of Greek myths

120 pp. (1959, Reprint 2003) Paperback, ISBN 978-0-86516-309-6